TURN RIGHT AT DEATH VALLEY

BY

JOHN N. MERRILL

TURN RIGHT AT DEATH VALLEY
BY
JOHN N. MERRILL

Maps and photographs by John N. Merrill

a J.N.M. PUBLICATION

1986

Cover photograph—John Merrill near Death Hollow, Utah.

a J.N.M. PUBLICATION

J.N.M.PUBLICATIONS, WINSTER, MATLOCK, DERBYSHIRE DE4 2DQ

Conceived, editied, typest and designed by John N. Merrill.

First published September 1986

ISBN 0 907496 26 1

Typeset in Congress Regular and Congress Bold
Pointsize: 11 point   Linespace: 12 point

Typsetting interfaced by:
Steve Rothwell Typsetting Services, 20 St Ann's Square, Manchester, M2 7HG

Printed by:
Derbyshire Print
Station Road
Chesterfield
Derbyshire

ABOUT JOHN N. MERRILL

John combines the characteristics and strength of a mountain climber with the stamina, and athletic capabilities of a marathon runner. In this respect he is unique and has to his credit a whole string of remarkable long walks. He is without question the world's leading marathon walker.

Over the last ten years he has walked more than 55,000 miles and successfully completed ten walks of at least 1,000 miles or more.

His six walks in Britain are—

Hebridean Journey .... 1,003 miles
Northern Isles Journey .... 913 miles
Irish Island Journey .... 1,578 miles
Parkland Journey .... 2,043 miles
Lands End to John O'Groats .... 1,608 miles

and in 1978 he became the first person (permanent Guinness Book Of Records entry) to walk the entire coastline of Britain—6,824 miles in ten months.

In Europe he has walked across Austria (712 miles), hiked the Tour of Mont Blanc and GR20 in Corsica as training! In 1982 he walked across Europe—2,806 miles in 107 days—crossing seven countries, the Swiss and French Alps and the complete Pyrennean chain—the hardest and longest mountain walk in Europe.

In America he used the world's longest footpath—The Appalachian Trail (2,200 miles) as a training walk. The following year he walked from Mexico to Canada in record time—118 days for 2,700 miles.

During the summer of 1984, John set off from Virginia Beach on the Atlantic coast, and walked 4,226 miles without a rest day, across the width of America to San Francisco and the Pacific Ocean. This walk is unquestionably his greatest achievement, being, in modern history, the longest, hardest crossing of the USA in the shortest time—under six months (177 days). The direct distance is 2,800 miles.

Between major walks John is out training in his own area —the Peak District National Park. As well as walking in other areas of Britain and in Europe he has been trekking in the Himalayas four times. He lectures extensively and is author of more than sixty books.

CONTENTS

TURN RIGHT AT DEATH VALLEY

INTRODUCTION

I had been aware since the early 70's of the tremendous scope in America for long distance walking. But first I had to extensively walk my own country, to develop my skills and establish myself in my unusual career. I walked over 20,000 miles, and successfully completed six walks over 1,000 miles long. The last, in 1978, was the first circumnavigation of the British coastline—6,824 miles in ten months. I now felt ready to tackle walks in America.

My first walk, in 1979, was along the Appalachian Trail. The world's longest trail, from Springer Mountain in Georgia to Mt. Katahdin in Maine, via fourteen States. At the time the trail was said to be 2,034 miles long. Based on my experience, I walk a 1,000 miles in a maximum of 40 days. I therefore booked my flights and allowed 90 days for the trail. It soon became obvious that the trail was much longer than thought. I know I walked 2,200 miles, but because of my time scale I had to miss 150 miles of trail in Maine. I am convinced that the trail is 2,400 miles long.

However, disappointed as I was not to do all the trail, I had done what I had set out to do. To walk 2,000 miles in America as a training walk in preparation for future walks. One aspect that I did not appreciate at the time was my deep love for America. I returned home stunned by what I had seen.

Eight months later I was back, in May 1980, to tackle a trail I first read about ten years earlier in the National Geographic magazine—The Pacific Crest Trail. The trail runs from the Mexican border through California, Oregon and Washington State to Manning Park, just inside British Columbia, Canada. The route is 2,500 miles long, and traverses the remotest terrain in North America. For scenery I know of no other major walk that has the variety and majestic splendour. Nor too is it usually possible to walk for fourteen days and not see another human being.

When I started I failed to appreciate that the guidebooks were written for American walkers who average 14 miles a day. Since I average twice as much, I reached certain areas too soon. The High Sierras were swamped in snow—200% more than usual. I tried to get through, but the trail lay under 15 feet of snow. In the end I took the alternative route along Highway 395 in the Owen's Valley. After 2,000 miles of walking I reached the Columbia river on the Oregon and Washington State line. Here the route was closed to Mount Rainier because of the eruption of Mt. St. Helen's, three months previously.

I headed west to Portland and the Pacific Coast and walked the Oregon Coast Trail to Astoria, at the mouth of the Columbia river. Across the river I headed for the Olympic Peninsula before crossing Pueget Sound to Seattle and onto Mt. Rainier. I reached Canada two weeks later, after walking 2,700 miles in 118 days. I flew immediately back to the Owen's Valley and ascended Mt. Whitney—at 14,496 feet the highest point in the lower 48 States and just off the Pacific Crest Trail.

After five months in America I flew home, humbled at what I had done and shattered at leaving America. I had grown even fonder of the country, and for three months I was very disorientated. Eighteen months were to pass before I felt accustomed to British life.

I felt I could not go back again in 1981, although I wanted to walk the Continental Divide Trail—3,100 miles along the Rockies from the Mexican border to Canada. My mind kept thinking about doing my own coast to coast walk, for I had walked the eastern and western sides, but what was there in the middle? I pencilled in 1982 in my diary for this, but a nagging thought of Europe kept popping into my thoughts. I had done little there, but the Alps and Pyreneean chain were appealing. By the time 1982 arrived I had a plan to walk from the North Sea to the Mediterranean via Holland, Belgium, Luxembourg, the Swiss and French Alps to Nice. I knew that would be about 1,600 miles, and not long enough for me! I therefore continued round the Riviera to Spain and crossed the Pyrenees from coast to coast. The walk was the longest and hardest mountain walk possible in Europe—2,800 miles in 107 days!

I returned to Britain happy but wondering what next? America loomed again, and the Continental Divide. I decided 1983 was the year for this, but worried about my reactions to being back in the States. I needn't have worried; it felt like returning home. But it was not to prove my year. There was an unusual amount of snow in Montana, and the trail was not possible. I road-walked round, but another problem occurred—marauding grizzly bears. Again the trails were closed. After a person had been eaten alive, I decided it was wiser to withdraw.

I felt a great loss at returning, but decided that in 1984 I would be back again to walk from coast to coast. Direct it is 2,800 miles, but I don't do anything direct! I worked out a 177 day schedule, with a daily average of 24 miles per day, and on paper 4,250 miles long. My calculations were correct, and I walked 4,226 miles in 177 days.

Although I write this ten days after my return to England, I still cannot appreciate what I have accomplished. It was a dream through unforgettable scenery, amidst the friendliest people on earth. The following is the story of the walk.

John N. Merrill.

John N. Merrill.

Winster. November 1984.

HOW IT WAS DONE

THE ROUTE —

I looked at a general map of America for a long time, arguing the pro's and con's for specific crossings. Eventually I decided that by using Latitude 40 degrees as a base line, I would pass through numerous National Parks and scenic areas. Coupled with the fact that there was a monument at Cape Henry recording the landing of the British in 1607; my start was arranged.

Basically the route had to be as hard as possible, with options all the time to take advantage of good weather. At the same time I wanted it to be the 'grand slam' of America. I spent days breaking my idea down into a daily schedule of 177 days. For the first part of the route I headed almost due west, not because the scenery was dull but simply I felt psychologically it was better to have a good distance under the belt early before weaving my way all over to visit specific areas.

My principal route was
Virginia: Appalachian Trail and mountains, Cumberland Historical Park.
Kentucky: Mammoth Cave National Park and Land between the Lakes.
Missouri: Ozarks.
Kansas: Dodge City and Santa Fe Trail.
Colorado: Continental Divide/Rockies and Mesa Verde National Park.
Utah: Five National Parks—Canyonlands, Arches, Capitol Reef, Bryce Canyon, and Zion.
Arizona: Grand Canyon National Park.
Nevada: Hoover Dam, Las Vegas and desert.
California: Death Valley National Monument, High Sierras and Yosemite National Park.

San Francisco was the obvious conclusion to the route, but because of the maze of interstate highways I decided Monterey Bay and Santa Cruz were more appropriate. I then walked up Highway 1 to San Francisco.

The whole route was worked out on general State maps, and although I avoid it as much as possible usually, it would have to be road walking much of the way. On past experience I have walked up to 3,700 miles without a rest day, and averaging 25 to 28 miles per day. I was very conscious of overstretching myself and having bones break because I had walked too much. I decided that an average of 24 miles overall would alleviate the problem. It did, and although I was tired and lost 30 lbs. in weight, I had no serious foot trouble. The schedule worked out to be 177 days long. I decided that May 15th would be the day to start, so that I would not meet snow in the Appalachians. I did'nt, but the temperature was below freezing at night. My main worry were the High Sierras. Would I get there in mid-October, and before the snow? In the event I did'nt, and only just got through. One thing I was determined not to do, and that was to read up about the areas I would be passing through. Simply, I wanted to get to the places uninformed and 'discover for myself'. Had I known how much heat I would endure, I might never have set off!

EQUIPMENT

I spent several months testing and evaluating equipment. Originally I hoped to use all British-made products, but in the end there were none suitable or that I had confidence would last. I therefore used American-made equipment, none of which let me down.

BOOTS—I have never approved of the so-called 'lightweight boot' revolution. From past experience a top-quality hiking boot, whatever its weight, is far superior to lightweight. I wanted to use a pair of lightweight boots as an experiment on the walk. After extensively trying seven pairs, I selected an all-leather pair. On the walk they lasted 700 miles, and caused daily pain and blisters. They were the worst pair I have ever worn on a major walk. They conclusively proved that they are quite unsuitable for multiple day walking. I changed back into so-called 'heavy-weight' boots. Immediately I had cushioning off the ground, ample ankle support and no blisters or sore feet. The first pair lasted 2,000 miles and were heeled only. In Telluride, Colorado, I bought a new pair, weighing 5 lbs., and they saw me through the final 1,750 miles, with a resole at 1,400 miles. Apart from occasionally applying Neatsfoot Oil, they were rarely oiled despite desert heat and 4½ months of 90 plus temperatures. To break in new boots while on the walk, I simply wore the new pair until they hurt, before changing back to the old pair. Usually after ten days the new boots were comfortable and the old pair were posted home as a souvenir!

TENT— My American-made tent weighed just over 4 lbs.. It was the first time I have used a tent twice on major walks. Generally I buy a new one each time, but this tent has been used in the Himalayas, Europe and America. I can't find anything better! Made out of gore-tex, it leaked on the seams, but was otherwise faultless. I would have liked to have camped out more, but in many areas the police did not advise me to camp alone and by a road.

RUCKSACK— This is one item that does only last one walk. My American-made sack was faded and worn all over at the end. I carried between 40 and 50 lbs., depending on how much food I had. Even after 177 days I still knew I had a weight on my back. It was always comfortable and stable, with an internal frame and a capacity of 80 litres.

CLOTHING— Socks were always wearing out; one pair after 3 days. Where possible I used 80% wool socks, and on average they lasted three weeks before being worn out on the heels. I wore shorts all the time, and the first pair lasted five months. T-shirts on top—my second one was bought in Missouri, and by the time I reached the Pacific it was collapsing; but I get very attached to my shirts! I set off with a fleece-lined jacket, but after a couple of weeks of 95o weather I sent it back. I bought a sweatshirt five months later for the High Sierras, and wore it only twice. I had a gore-tex suit made for the rain, but after seven suits I still remain very unconvinced of its properties. Thankfully, I had little rain, and on the five occasions I put the suit on I sweated profusely and felt very uncomfortable. In the end it had to rain very hard before I put it on. At other times I walked in the rain and became sodden rather than suffer the unpleasantness of the jacket and trousers. With being in the sun so much, I had to wear a small cap occasionally, for my forehead and head were frequently burnt and peeling. I hate anything on my head, and the cap was used with great reluctance.

FOOD AND COOKING— I carried an MSR stove, and used it only once. Being such hot weather, I preferred to eat a salad than cook a hot meal. Eating out is way of life in America, and when I could I had a large breakfast of ham or bacon with two eggs 'over-easy', hash browns, toast and jelly, and a minimum of three cups of coffee. During the day I ate little, but when I could I had a litre of milk, and on a few occasions I drank a gallon of milk! Salad for dinner, but, in towns, hamburgers, liver or steak were the norm. I was conscious of the amount of burgers I ate, and in the first month I had consumed over forty. I eased off, and ended up by eating about 150. I was aware also of caffeine, and tried to drink caffeine-free drinks, but I still consumed 460 cans of Coke or Dr. Pepper! I never took into account the calorific or protein content of my food. I simply ate what I wanted, and often after a steak would munch my way through a couple of packets of 'M & M's'. Walking, to me, is mental exercise, and nothing to do with calorific values.

TRAINING

One would immediately surmise that extensive training was necessary or even imperative for such an undertaking. However, I did nothing! This was on purpose, for from experience I have trained and found that after 500 miles I was beginning to settle down on the walk; after 1,000 miles I would be reasonably fit; after 1,500 miles I could take everything in my stride, and at 2,000 miles I would be at peak performance. I would remain at this high pitch for 500 miles before beginning to decline.

Since I would be walking further than I have ever walked before without a rest day, I decided not to train and become fit. Instead I planned on being very unfit, so that the first weeks would see me getting fit while on the actual walk. I assumed, correctly, that I would peak later. I did, at 2,500 miles, and kept in reasonably top performance for a further 1,000 miles. The final 750 miles were very ragged. One day I would walk well and do 26 miles, and the next I would struggle to walk 20 miles. By the time I reached the coast I was extremely weary—more tired mentally and physically than ever before—and showed no emotion at seeing the Pacific.

There was one further reason for lack of training. On my British Coastal Walk, after 3,000 miles a bone snapped in my foot; simply from walking too much. I was averaging 28 miles per day with 60 lbs. of equipment. I planned to walk 24 miles per day in an attempt to overcome any possible foot problems. I had none, except the usual blistered sore feet at the beginning. Whilst I worried about only walking 24 miles per day, I found it no problem as I was road walking—which is much harder, because the ground does not 'give', than trail walking.

CAMERA

I carried just one 35 mm. camera with a wide angle zoom lens—50 mm. to 28 mm. For flower shots and special views I used a 80 × 210 mm. zoom lens. I always find it hard to make myself stop and photograph myself. I carried a small tripod for this, but rarely found a post to strap it to or a suitable rock to stand it on. Instead, I simply put the camera on top of my pack and kept running backwards and forwards, setting the delayed action and smiling in time before the shutter clicked. I used basically Kodachrome slide film 25 ASA and 64 ASA. On a few occasions I used Ektachrome 100 ASA and 400 ASA; and some 100 ASA Fuji film. I was extremely anxious about developing the film as soon as possible, because of the hot temperatures I was walking in. I sent the Kodak film to Britain for processing and mounting, and the rest was processed locally and sent to Britain. I took about 3,000 colour slides, and not one film was lost or damaged.

COST

Inevitably you will wonder what such an undertaking cost. I sought no sponsorship, nor did I receive any. I tend not to budget, feeling that I have enough worries just to do the walk and deal with the normal running problems. I had the blessing of my local Bank Manager, and instead of carrying a lot of money I simply called at an American Express office and cashed a cheque. The walk—including air-fares, accommodation, meals, film, postage and equipment—came to £6,000 ($8,000). When one considers it was a six month trip, I feel the cost was relatively cheap.

WATER

I tend to break all the accepted rules of walking, including going alone; telling no-one my route, and carrying no water. Only on a handful of occasions did I carry any, despite the desert country I would be passing through. I have learnt from experience that once you start to drink water you want more and more. I would rather abstain, and often went 10 to 12 hours without drinking. I found this no hardship. Since I generally walk twice as far as an American backpacker every day, I knew I would reach water frequently. My further objection to water is carrying it! I consider I have enough on my back without adding further weight.

CARS

Being on roads much of the time, you are bound to wonder whether I took a lift. I always kept to the lefthand edge of the road and faced the oncoming traffic. No more than twenty cars stopped to offer a lift. Two actually drove back to me, and although I refused we had a long conversation beside the road, on the 'story so far'. On a few occasions I hitched a lift to get to a bank, post office, film processor, or campsite. But, I always returned to my pickup point the next day. I had no backup party, so I had little idea of what amenities lay ahead. At a couple of places I had to get a ride simply to get food, only to discover that it was only three miles away. Even people locally did not know what was just ahead.

PEOPLE

The American image is taken from the T.V. screen. Whereas in reality the people are extremely friendly, helpful, and often go right out of their way to help. I had no unpleasant experience along the route coast to coast. I could walk into the best motel in shorts and T-shirt and be treated with considerable civility. I saw few guns, and in the countryside the houses would be open and the car keys left in the car.

GETTING THERE

On May 12th, 1984, I flew to Washington D.C.. Before actually starting the walk, I felt it was only right that I visited the nation's capital. Although shattered by jet lag, before falling asleep I quickly walked down from my hotel near Farragut Square and saw the White House!

The following morning, after breakfast in a Roy Rogers restaurant—the only one I saw on the entire walk—I began exploring Washington on foot in my boots and shorts. First another look at the White House, before ascending the Washington Column and its extensive view over the Capitol, Mall and river. From my vantage point I worked out my route up the Mall to the museums, the Hoover building (FBI headquarters), the Capitol and both the Senate and House of Representatives' Chambers, and the walk back to the Abraham Lincoln Memorial and the new Vietnam War Memorial. I would have liked to have seen more, but that little lot took all day! By far the most impressive feature of the day was the NASA Museum and film show on early flight. The film was unnerving, being shown on a screen at least 100 feet wide and 50 feet high. You really felt you were there in the planes as they dived and wheeled through the air. Often I gripped my seat, expecting to fall out as we plummeted earthwards.

The next morning I took the subway to the airport, and half an hour later I boarded a 'plane for Norfolk in Virginia. By early afternoon I had checked into a beach-fronted motel—an 'Econo Lodge', whose tartan motto said "Spend a night not a fortune". My Scottish wife would have been amused. The weather was warm and, although not officially summer yet, the beach was full of bronzed bodies and bikini-clad girls. The waves gently broke on the sandy shore. Close to the motel I found a sign saying 'London 3,718 miles and San Francisco miles 2,519".

I was at the start: I wondered what would happen over the coming months. Would I make it? Would there be snow in the Appalachians? What would Missouri and Kansas be like? Could I cross Grand Canyon and the infamous Death Valley? Would I be able to cross the High Sierras before snow fell? Perhaps most of all, would my feet stand up to it? I didn't really appreciate that my greatest walk was about to begin. I was simply excited but nervous about what was going to happen. I slept fitfully that night.

WHITE HOUSE FROM WASHINGTON COLUMN

LINCOLN MEMORIAL FROM WASHINGTON COLUMN

VIRGINIA BEACH

VIRGINIA

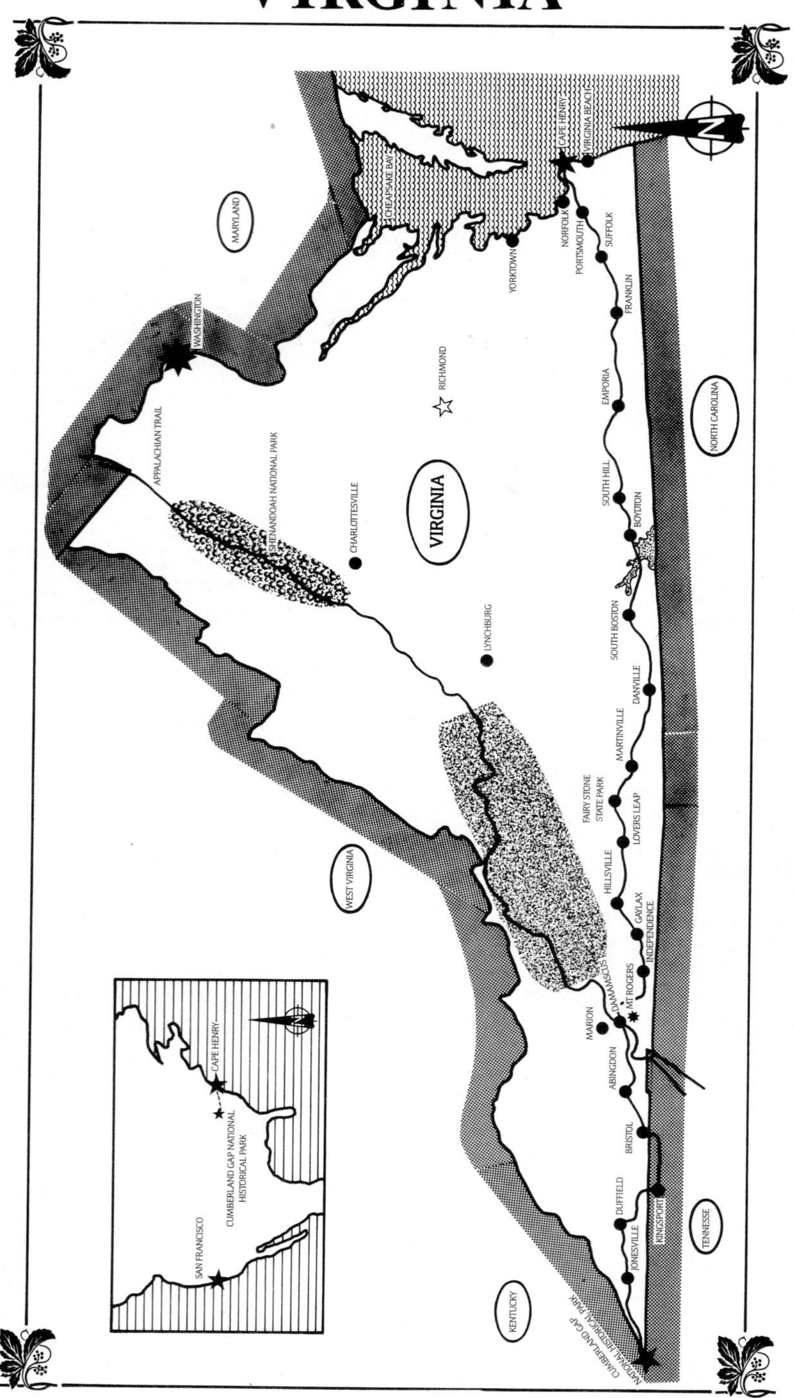
MARYLAND
WASHINGTON
CHEAPSAKE BAY
CAPE HENRY
VIRGINIA BEACH
NORFOLK
PORTSMOUTH
SUFFOLK
YORKTOWN
FRANKLIN
RICHMOND
EMPORIA
NORTH CAROLINA
APPALACHIAN TRAIL
SHENANDOAH NATIONAL PARK
CHARLOTTESVILLE
VIRGINIA
SOUTH HILL
BOYDTON
LYNCHBURG
SOUTH BOSTON
DANVILLE
MARTINVILLE
FAIRY STONE STATE PARK
LOVERS LEAP
HILLSVILLE
GAYLAX
INDEPENDENCE
WEST VIRGINIA
DAMASCUS
MT ROGERS
MARION
ABINGDON
BRISTOL
KINGSPORT
DUFFIELD
JONESVILLE
TENNESSEE
KENTUCKY
CUMBERLAND GAP NATIONAL HISTORICAL PARK
CAPE HENRY
CUMBERLAND GAP NATIONAL HISTORICAL PARK
SAN FRANCISCO

VIRGINIA — THE OLD DOMINION

CAPITAL — RICHMOND

POPULATION (1980 CENSUS) - 5,346,279

HIGHEST ELEVATION — MT. ROGERS IN THE APPALACHIANS, 5,729 FEET.

LOWEST ELEVATION — SEA LEVEL

TOTAL AREA — 40,815 SQUARE MILES.

DAY 1— CAPE HENRY TO PORTSMOUTH—23 MILES

I was up early, and eating my first large American breakfast before 7.00 a.m.. I didn't stint myself, eating a couple of eggs 'over-easy', rashers of bacon, sausages and hash browns, swilled down with several cups of caffeine-filled coffee. Feeling wide awake, I boarded the bus to Cape Henry, the true start of the walk, ten miles away. By the time we reached the entrance gates to Fort Story, where the Cape is, I was the only passenger and rather shell-shocked as to what was about to happen.

Shouldering my load for the first time, I walked to the memorial just beside the sea, with a cross nearby marking the approximate place where on April 26th, 1607, the first permanent American settlers touched American soil. They then moved on to found Jamestown. There was no-one around to take my photograph, so I walked down to the shore to see the Atlantic for the last time. I stood with the seawater lapping my boots and prayed for the strength needed to overcome the obstacles that lay ahead to the Pacific Ocean.

I retraced my steps back to the cross and monument, and saw a tourist reading the sign. I asked him if he would photograph me with my camera, which he did, and glibly told him I was setting off to walk across America. I am convinced he didn't appreciate what I was about to do. He simply shook me by the hand and wished me well, before getting into his beloved Chevrolet and hitting the tarmac. I too began to walk along the edge of the road, on the left facing the oncoming traffic. There was very little, and two hours later I reached the entrance gates of the Fort, complete with sentry. He was startled to see someone walking, especially with a fifty pound pack. Again I casually mentioned that I was now heading west to walk across America—4,250 miles in 177 days. "Should reach San Francisco on November 8th!", I told him. He remained speechless, and just mouthed—"You are going to walk?" I left him leaning against the wall shaking his head.

I had now reached my first highway (60), which I basically followed to Norfolk, part of which I had ridden along from the airport to Virginia Beach. After ten miles I could feel my feet getting sore, and the hot sun had already reddened my neck and head. There was such a conglomeration of roads that I eventually ended up taking the wrong one, with a bridge then tunnel to Portsmouth. I checked with the Highway Patrol, and they said I could walk over the bridge. But once over I could not walk through the tunnel. I stood at the entrance wondering what to do, when a car pulled up and took me through the tunnel to the other side. There I resumed my walk into Portsmouth. On my right was Norfolk Naval Base, the largest in the world and home to more than 110 ships of the Atlantic and Mediterranean fleets.

By now it was early evening, and my face was beetroot and my feet were in agony. I simply walked on: to stop would have been fatal. Two miles later I reached a motel—another 'Econo-Lodge'. Five minutes later I was in my room and lying in a hot bath. Both feet were badly blistered; two blisters were 1½ inches in diameter. Never before have my feet hurt so much. I limped off for a steak, before ringing Sheila to let her know I had begun.

JOHN MERRILL AT CAPE HENRY

DAY 2—
PORTSMOUTH TO SUFFOLK—
22 MILES (45 MILES)

I left the motel just after 6.00 a.m., refreshed and with my blisters feeling quite comfortable. A mile up the road I stopped at a restaurant for breakfast. I ate another large breakfast while the cook and waitress learnt about my walk. When I came to pay the bill they would not accept anything, saying it was "on them" and wishing me the best of luck. I carried on along Highway 337, moving away from the built-up areas and entering quiet, flat countryside with fields and little traffic.

After ten miles I reached Driver, and sat beside the road debating what to do. I had intended to keep on small roads, but soon realised that this would bring me to few amenities. I also fully appreciated I was unfit and, on reaching Driver, very tired. This was partly because of my lack of training and the hot weather—80°F. already in mid-May. I decided the wisest route was on more major highways, while I settled down to the task. I therefore headed south-west to Suffolk, the largest city in Virginia.

The whole region, whilst being established by the British, still bears the names of English places. Within thirty miles I had walked from Norfolk via Portsmouth to Suffolk. Ahead were the counties of the Isle of Wight, Southampton and Sussex. It was like walking through Britain in a few strides. It never ceased to surprise me how unoriginal Americans were about place names. I would walk through London later in Kentucky, and even Glasgow!

After eight hours of walking, I found a motel in Suffolk and flopped down exhausted. My feet were extremely sore, my legs had stiffened up, and, for the first time ever, my thigh ball sockets hurt. I wrote in my diary: "Do I cut weight or slow down?" I simply decided to see how I felt a week later, and, forgetting my problems, slipped into a hot bath for a long soak. After a meal, I was asleep by 6.00 p.m. and slept solidly for twelve hours.

NORFOLK DOCKS

DAY 3— SUFFOLK TO FRANKLIN— 23 MILES (68 MILES)

The third day of a major walk is always crucial to me—a sort of make or break day. I awoke feeling better and more my usual self, full of life and enthusiasm for the walk. Before setting off along Highway 58, Lynda McNab of the Suffolk News and Herald came for an interview and to take photographs. The interview went smoothly, but was interrupted by a car crash outside the motel. The ambulance appeared within seconds, and Lynda had to photograph the smashed-up car for the newspapers.

I strode on in good spirits; the press were at last taking an interest. My start had not been covered, as the Olympic torch also began its 9,000-mile journey that day across America to Los Angeles and the 23rd Olympiad. However, I felt in good shape, and decided to buy a further pair of insoles for my boots. Part of my foot problem was because I had wrongly assumed that a pair of leather lightweight boots would be suitable for the walk. But in reality they provided no ankle support; neither did they cushion my feet on the ground. I did not want another pair of boots yet, and decided to use these for a while. The extra insole certainly helped, and I walked much better, with my blisters starting to heal nicely.

My route was along the two-laned dual highway for twelve miles before I could go on the smaller business 58 Highway via Holland to Franklin. Suffolk was peanut country, and, as the city sign said: "We're nuts about Suffolk." Later I walked past the Hancock Peanut factory. I was now seeing many historical markers beside the road. One told me I was in Nansemond County, which was formed in 1637 and had an area of 423 square miles; it was named after an Indian tribe. In Holland I came to a marker recording that here on May 21, 1928, the first Ruritan Club was founded. The members are rural leaders and, like Rotary and other similar organisations, strive through community service, fellowship and goodwill to make the rural community a better place to live.

I reached Franklin tired but in good spirits, and knew I was on my way. I lay in my motel room and watched television. I soon became an addict—statistics say that although American schoolchildren have 2,500 hours of schooling a year, they watch 3,500 hours of television! Two programmes fascinated me. First was the Love Connection, which was on five days a week and rather like computer dating, with the couples explaining how they got on on their first date. If the audience agreed with the choice, they had another expenses-paid evening! The other was a simple quiz programme called Wheel of Fortune. Whilst the questions were easy, the amount of money they won was astounding.

SUFFOLK NUTS

DAY 4— FRANKLIN TO CAPRON— 23 MILES (91 MILES)

When I set off at 7.00 a.m. the temperature was 56°F. and later rose to 80°F. My skin, which had been bright pink so far, was noticeably changing to light brown. I left the Isle of Wight county (314 square miles), which was originally formed in 1634, and entered Southampton county. Later I would walk past the impressive pillared Southampton Courthouse. The houses in Franklin were very attractive, and very colonial in design; reminding me very much of the New England states. One wooden building with tower and porch all the way round the base was particularly eye-catching, and dated from about 1880. In a country where anything over 75 years is pulled down, it was good to see this very well cared-for house with manicured lawns.

The highway soon became just two-laned, and I enjoyed walking along the relatively flat countryside, with a few small hills scattered around, although I was only a few hundred feet above sea level. I was pleased with my walking pace—about three miles an hour— and that my feet were settling down. I was never lonely road-walking, and always kept my mind active. My prime topics of discussion with myself were my feet and boots. I now knew the hard way that, despite what the manufacturers claim, lightweight leather walking boots are totally unsuitable for a long-distance walk with a pack. Their only use is for day walking without a pack. My other topic was America. Already I was feeling very much at home, and wrote in my diary that night—"Why America? Because you have the freedom to do what you want, and no-one hassles you."

At Capron, I downed a pint of milk before asking around for somewhere to camp. I had reached one of those blank spots on the route, for no-one was very helpful and I walked on. Half a mile later, a car pulled up and gave me a lift to Emporia, where there was a motel. I hated getting in the car, but I had no option—the police had advised me not to camp alone beside the road. The next morning I would return to Capron.

SOUTHAMPTON COURT HOUSE

DAY 5— CAPRON TO EMPORIA— 20 MILES (111 MILES)

I was back in Capron by 7.00 a.m., and it was already warm. I pressed on along Highway 58 for Emporia, my final day of level walking; beyond Emporia the hills began. The walking was very pleasant, being a mixture of trees and fields and few cars. I had now been in America a week, although it already seemed months. Three hours later, with ten miles walked, it was becoming appreciably hotter. I hate wearing anything on my head, but thinning hair is beginning to make it necessary in the sun. With great reluctance I put on my cap. When I reached the downtown area of Emporia shortly after 1.00 p.m., the temperature sign in the mall read 91°F. No wonder I was sweating.

I stayed at the Holiday Inn, the only motel there. It never ceased to amaze me how I was treated wherever I went. In Britain, if a hiker walked into the lobby of some high-class hotel with a pack on his back, he would be told politely to leave or that no rooms were available. But in America it is very different. I would walk into the best motels in my boots, heavy pack and sweaty T-shirt, and be instantly given a room. I would, of course, explain what I was doing, and often I would have the room at a substantial discount or business rate. I had never intended to stay in motels quite so much at the start, but there was no alternative.

Just down from the motel was the classic American street with a whole line of fast food places—Hardees, McDonalds, Wendy's and Pizza Hut. I headed for McDonalds, and tucked into a big Mac, french fries and a delicious strawberry milk shake. In the mall I bought sun-tan lotion, which I used spasmodically over the next six months. I never could get into the habit of putting on the cream every morning before I started. Had I done so, my nose and forehead would not have been in a continuous peeling state.

Back at the motel I met the local reporter and gave her the story so far. She took photographs of me outside with my shining new pack. It is interesting to look at the photographs now and realise how within a week I had changed from being almost white in colour to being a sun-tanned and muscular young man—I was only forty! Shortly after the photo session a Greyhound bus passed—destination Los Angeles. 172 days for me; three for them.

The T.V. news was full of items on Utah—I would be there in four months, in September. The Rockies had had more than 200% more snow than usual, and with the sudden rise in temperature—I was now in the midst of a heatwave, and it was not officially summer yet—the snow was melting rapidly. Large areas were flooded, and several large mud slides had occurred. Quite a disaster area. I rang Sheila to report on my first week in America.

WENDYS AND MACDONALDS

DAY 6—EMPORIA TO BRODNAX—34 MILES (145 MILES)

Shortly after 7.00 a.m. I crossed Interstate 95, and kept on my faithful Highway 58. It was already hot, and I had attached a small thermometer to my shoulder strap, where it remained for the rest of the walk enabling me to record the daily high's. By 10 a.m. it was over 80°F., and over 90°F. by 1.00 p.m.. The road was a dual-laned highway with gentle hills ahead. Perhaps the most worrying aspect was the straightness of the road. This aspect of American walking always made me nervous in planning the walk. How would I react to seeing a straight road anything up to twenty miles ahead? Would it simply demoralise me? I overcame the problem quite simply by subconsciously noting I could see far ahead but only concentrating on the ground immediately ahead. I never looked back to see how far I had come. My morale was always high as a result. I was often asked: 'Why road-walk?', but there is no alternative. No trails went my way, but as someone remarked: 'Our roads are our trails.'

Near Eggerton I stopped at a store and hamburger joint. I was carrying no food, but decided to purchase a few items for emergency. Before leaving I ate another hamburger, my thirteenth so far! I kept on the highway as it by-passed Lawrencefield—just as well I didn't stop there, for everything was closed, being a Sunday. The heat was now at its peak, yet I felt fit and strong, quite a change from a week ago. I never intended to walk so far this day, but there was no alternative and nowhere to stay. After 12½ hours, I reached Brodnax feeling quite shattered. A bad blister was developing on my left heel, which I had ignored for the last five miles. The heat in the end had sapped me, and while I rested I drank my way through six cans of ice-cold coke.

HIGHWAY 58 AND MY FIRST HILL!

DAY 7— BRODNAX TO RUDDS CREEK CAMPGROUND—29 MILES (174 MILES)

I felt tired from yesterday's big push, and after crossing Interstate 85, headed for South Hill on Highway 58. I debated whether to stop there, but decided I would feel guilty having an 'easy day', so carried on to Boydton, nineteen miles away. After a couple of miles the road became single lane and not much traffic. I limped along with my left heel very sore, but I am too stubborn to stop. The heat was already making inroads in my determination, and by early afternoon was in the mid-90's F.. I kept enquiring how far Boydton was—"just a few miles—you will be there in an hour!". I hated asking, for it was always demoralising, but also it clearly indicated that they had no idea how far it was, being so car-orientated.

I reached Boydton after nine hours of walking. I should have stopped here, but there was no motel. The nearest place was a campground three miles ahead. I decided to stop there, and after purchasing some food and strawberries and cream, for a treat, headed for the campground. Being early season there was only a handful of people camping. I paid my five dollar fee and camped in the trees close to the shore of Rudds Creek.

Behind me was a trailer, and the sole occupier came to see me. Obviously he was curious to see a solitary hiker, and didn't grasp the fact that I had walked from the Atlantic. It soon became obvious that his attention wasn't out of curiosity but sexual. I asked him what he did, and with his right hand moving around in his trouser pocket he replied: "I play with myself." He invited me back to camp for a chicken leg on his bar-b-que, followed by a visit to his trailer. I refused. He wandered off to visit another "friend", while I put the tent up and enjoyed a soothing and prolonged hot shower.

On my way back to the tent, he was waiting. "Come and have a chicken leg", he called. I refused again, and sat at my table and enjoyed a sardine salad, followed by strawberries. The strawberries reminded me of my 2,800 mile walk in Europe two years ago. There every night I had camped out, and for six weeks ate a pound of strawberries every evening! My neighbour visited me again, with peace offerings this time. A glass of Kentucky bourbon and, symbolically, a couple of bananas! He knew he had offended me, but was still hopeful I would visit him. I didn't.

BOYDTON

DAY 8—RUDDS CREEK TO CLARKSVILLE—12 MILES (186 MILES)

I had an undisturbed night, and was walking by 7.00 a.m. before my solicitous friend was around. I felt very sluggish, and knew I had pushed it too much too soon—I never learn. I decided I would stop at Clarksville. I very soon crossed Rudds Creek, which is a minor arm of the huge John H. Kerr dam and reservoir, being built by the Corps of Engineers, Wilmington district of North Carolina, in 1953. The reservoir is 39 miles long, covers 50,000 acres and has an 800-mile shoreline. Part of the area was controlled by the Occoneechee Indians, who lived here and traded furs until they were dispersed in 1676 by Nathaniel Bacon, the Rebel.

Before I crossed the final major bridge to Clarksville, I passed a huge election sign to Virginia's senator, John Warner, one of Elizabeth Taylor's ex-husbands. I stayed at a motel overlooking the lake. To make life easier I had decided to sort my rucksack out and send back anything I didn't really need. I cut everything to the minimum, and sent back my spare shorts, T-shirts and fibre-pile jacket—a total of five pounds. The pile jacket was intended for the Appalachians and cold weather, but with temperatures into the 90's already, I decided correctly that I would not need it.

While I was in the Post Office mailing the clothes back, I met the local writer, Gail Bradley, who wrote novels and children's books. She quickly rushed round to the offices of the Sun newspaper, and they agreed to accept a story from her. She took me to her home overlooking the lake, and, while I tucked into a huge salad sandwich, she interviewed me.

To my amazement, I decided to wash my clothes—something I rarely do. I sat in the laundramat and washed everything. To complete my lazy afternoon, I ate my way through a large rib-eye steak and drank a couple of bottles of Micelob beer—I felt I deserved it.

RUDDS CREEK

DAY 9—CLARKSVILLE TO SOUTH BOSTON—23 miles (209 miles)

Feeling refreshed from yesterday's easy day I was tucking into three hot cakes smothered in maple syrup at 6.0 am. Half an hour later I was walking in an effort to get a good mileage covered before the heat made itself felt. Yesterday it had been in the 90's again, but I needn't have worried for it never did get too hot—80°F at the most. Another surprise was rain—not hard but just a steady drizzle for a couple of hours. I christened my gore-tex jacket, but soon found it kept the rain out and the perspiration in; I was soaked inside.

I walked along Highway 58, a two-laned highway which thankfully was not too busy. The countryside, although still flat, had lost its built-up look as I moved into farming country with facilities far apart. The road was straight for long sections, but I did not find this off-putting. I ignored the road ahead and just walked, and it always surprised me how quickly I reached my destination. To let my mind dwell on the huge distances and the long straight roads would have been disastrous to my mental approach—I would have been put off. Better to concentrate on my immediate area and appreciate what I could see. Whilst my boots were totally inadequate for the walk and my feet were still sore, at least they were not getting worse and my blisters were now healing.

Instead of going into South Boston, I kept on Highway 58 hoping I would find a motel, so I could go out live on my local Radio Station, BBC Radio Sheffield in England. After walking 23 miles I reached the aptly named Ridge Crest Motel and was made most welcome. The cost too was a pleasant surprise, only $19. The owners were most interested in my walk and contacted the local newspaper. Within ten minutes Ian Chandler, from the South Boston Gazette, arrived and spent an hour interviewing, and photographing my feet.

Afterwards I slipped into a hot bath to soak my battered feet. Moments later all hell let loose as a storm just erupted out of nowhere. It never ceased to amaze me how swiftly a storm moved in. Lightning and thunder crashed all around as the rain sheeted down. The gutters couldn't stand it and water just spewed all over and the tarmaced road became a flooded pond. Within half an hour the black clouds and rain had gone and the sun came out.

HIGHWAY 58

DAY 10—SOUTH BOSTON TO DANVILLE—33 miles (242 miles)

Just after 6.0 am I made my radio-link up and went out live on the programme. It felt very strange talking to England 4,000 miles away. I agreed to phone again in two weeks, but as the weeks passed and as I crossed time zones it became harder to make contact both mentally and practically. In the end I would have had to have been up at 3.0 a.m. I hurriedly ate a large breakfast of two eggs over-easy, ham, and toast and jelly. Ahead of me was 29 miles of dual highway walking to the next city, Danville.

At first it was cool, but the sun soon came out and the temperature rose to 90 degrees. But I felt comfortable and growing more accustomed to the heat and not being hindered by it. For the first time too my feet felt better and not nearly so tired as before. The walk took much longer than expected—11 hours to walk 33 miles. I was finding to my cost that the road maps gave inaccurate mileages between cities. The mileages only referred to the distance from city limit to city limit and not to the distance between them. In time I would walk several hundred more miles to reach a certain point than planned originally.

However, after 33 miles and well into Danville I came to my first motel, a Holiday Inn. I was tired from one of my longest day's walks so far, and accepted the luxury of a king-sized bed and a free breakfast. I ate a lasagne that night with a glass of Californian wine to celebrate the half-way point in Virginia.

HOUSE, FARM AND MAIL BOXES

DAY 11—DANVILLE TO COLLINSVILLE—32 miles (274 miles)

As I walked out of Danville, I appreciated its location beside the Dan River and searched in vain for the building near Main Street, the last Capital of the Confederacy. Again it was hot, into the 90's as I continued along the two-laned Highway 58 towards Martinsville. Again it was longer than I had thought, 25 miles I thought but this turned out to be 32 miles. Although the road was often straight for three or four miles at a time, I now had the added attraction of it being hilly country with a few hills to ascend. I was approaching the Appalachian foothills and knew that this was the last day of major highways as I neared the mountains and smaller places.

After nearly 20 miles I reached a gas station near Axton in mid-afternoon. I downed a couple of ice cold cokes while the owner explained that there were no motels in Martinsville. He proved extremely helpful and said there was a Holiday Inn in Collinsville, my nearest motel. I rang them and booked a room, explaining to a somewhat disbelieving receptionist that I was on foot. My friend drew a map of how to get to it and I set off again in renewed spirits.

Three hours later I reached Martinsville, feeling quite tired. Spotting a Hardees I walked in and sat down to a roast beef sandwich and a strawberry shake. I hadn't been sitting there long when a Virginian, who had been eyeing me for a while, came over with his wife and baby. He was a keen hiker and had walked sections of the Appalachian Trail. Asking what I was doing he was impressed and wished he had the courage to do something like it. Moments later I learned he had read my book, Turn Right at Land's End, the story of my 6,824 mile walk around Britain. Alas he had to go to Roanoke. I changed into trainers for the final four miles to ease my feet, and reached the motel little over an hour later. I ate nothing, just drank four cokes and fell asleep.

JOHN MERRILL AFTER SEVEN DAYS

DAY 12—COLLINSVILLE TO FAIRY STONE STATE PARK—22 miles (296 miles)

I rang Sheila before I left to give her a progress report. After the biggest breakfast so far—two eggs, bacon, ham, hash browns, toast, jelly, orange juice and four cups of coffee—I was walking by 8.0 a.m. I decided after walking more than 30 miles on each of the last two days, I must ease off and not punish my feet so much. I began following Highway 57 past numerous furniture manufacturers in the Martinsville—Bassett area. Past these entered forest and quiet roads. Entering a small town outside the store they were having a sale for the local church. I stopped for a cake but was soon pressed to more food and drink, 'on the house'. Explaining my walk so far was rather like singing for my supper but they made me most welcome.

An hour later I was on my way, walking slowly for the effort of the last two days, at such an early part of the walk, began to make itself felt. I walked into the State Park and camped. The charge was $5 which at the time was about £4 sterling.

The park takes its name from the Fairy Stone, which is only found here in Patrick County. The stone is a Staurolites—a twinned staurolite crystal similar to a Maltese or St. Andrew's cross. I was given one the next day by the camp attendant.

> 'May the charms of the Fairy Stone make you blessed
> Through the days of labor and nights of rest
> Where ever you stay, where ever you go,
> May the beautiful Flowers of the good Fairies Grow.'

With the tent up beside a picnic table I walked down to the nearest shop, a mile away, to purchase some food. There was a shop on the site but it had been closed for more than a year! I bought salad ingredients and envisaged sitting outside and eating a tuna salad, but my hopes were dashed as I walked back to the tent in the rain. Shortly after getting there a thunderstorm burst across the area and I lay in the tent eating my salad and two vanilla puddings.

CAR DUMP

DAY 13—FAIRY STONE STATE PARK TO MEADOWS OF DAN— 25 miles (321 miles)

The storm and rain continued all night and I felt sorry for all those people who had been camping expecting better weather, for it was Memorial Weekend. A little after 7.0a.m. during a lull in the rain I packed the gear and set off. 100 yards later the rain sheeted down again and I sought shelter in the old shop. Moments later the camp attendant drove up and invited me to breakfast! While it poured and dripped off the trees as only in the Appalachians it can do, I devoured three hot cakes. My host gave me a fairy stone and explained the legend. It is said that before Christ was born the area was inhabited by fairies. Many years later the fairies were playing around a spring, when a messenger arrived informing them of the death of Christ. The fairies wept and their tears crystalised on the ground and formed crosses. It is these we find here today. It is the only place in the world where they are found and a 5,000 acre of land has been made into a State Park.

With my cross in my pocket—for luck—I left the camp attendant and made my way in the dull dry weather along Highway 57 to Cruzes Store. Here I could join my favourite Highway 58. I was now weaving my way through the Appalachian foothills, enjoying seeing a few hills and a lot of trees. At last I felt as though I was truly on my way as I began entering my first major obstacle and feature of the walk—the Appalachians.

From Cruzes Store I began ascending my first major hill; a 4½ mile road climb to Lovers Leap Overlook. Not that there was anything to see, for it was raining quite steadily and mist swirled around. It was cold too, only 50 degrees. A week ago it had been 95 degrees. On the rock beside the road numerous couples' names had been painted on. I descended, stopping frequently to see if I could see anything of the Appalachians, but saw nothing. Before I realised it I was out of the mist and saw the Blue Ridge Parkway sign. It felt quite strange to actually see a part of America that I had already been to before. The other side of the Parkway I checked into a Motel before walking back half a mile to eat. No one spoke much, perhaps they were startled to see a soaked hiker who had walked over Lover's Leap. I still had problems for I wrote in my log—Boots no good, feet still hurt.

FARM AND ROLLING HILL

DAY 14—
MEADOWS OF DAN TO HILLSVILLE—
22 miles (343 miles)

I had visions of walking up the Parkway to Mabry Mill to see the historic building and have breakfast there, but it was pouring with rain. In fact it rained all day, I little knew that this would be the last full day of rain for several months—not until a blizzard in California, five months ahead! I wore my Gore-tex jacket for the second time but although it kept the rain out it didn't breathe, I was again soaked inside.

I walked along Highway 58 enjoying the scenery which reminded me greatly of Britain, with fields, patches of woodland and generally hilly terrain. The people too were friendly, waving from their cars as they passed or speaking to me as I walked through Laurel Fork. I reached Hillsville early afternoon with tired feet. I soaked my feet in another hot bath and watched T.V. While I was in Washington I had visited the new Vietnam Memorial and much coverage was given in the news of an unknown Vietnam soldier being buried in Arlington Cemetry. At last the Vietnam War was being honoured, although the Americans seemed to find it hard to accept that they had been defeated.

DREAM HOUSE

DAY 15—HILLSVILLE TO GALAX—16 miles (359 miles)

I decided to have an easier day and stop at Galax as there would be nothing after there until Independence, a good 16 miles beyond. I was satisfied with my performance so far and was averaging 24 miles a day as planned. What still worried me were my feet and boots. Never had I experienced sore feet day after day, and never had I experienced being unable to push myself further if needed. In the end I concluded, that whilst I knew the boots were totally unsuitable, the continuous road walking was sapping my strength from the constant jarring of the surface. Never having experienced this before I was unaware of the strain it was placing on me. The thought of giving up never entered my mind.

I walked on Highway 58 across rolling hills and pleasant farms, reminding me of the Jura Alps in France. I had no alternative but to road walk for there were no trails going my way. The roadsides were full of colour with honeysuckle, rhododendrons and Dog Wood in bloom. The latter I was pleased so see, for it reminded me of my walk along the Appalachian Trail, five years ago. I stayed in Galax and purchased a new pair of insoles to give some kind of relief to my feet. I ate my first steak that night hoping it would give me some energy.

DOG WOOD FLOWER

DAY 16—GALAX TO INDEPENDENCE—16 miles (375 miles)

Following another Radio link up with Britain, I was walking by 7.0.a.m., following Highway 58 to Independence. I still felt tired, and with sore feet, but I was slowly beginning to take an interest in my surroundings. Extensive fields and wooded slopes of the Appalachians. Looking back now, after the walk, I realise just how tired I was in the early stages, more than I had ever been. It was a combinmation of heat, being unfit, and poor boots giving aching feet. I simply pressed on because of my determination, and my attention to my surroundings was clouded by my solitary drive. In time I would relax and become very aware of everything that I saw, but for the moment walked to get some distance behind me, which would boost my morale.

I reached Independence at midday and sat in a hamburger house and watched the world suddenly turn upside down. I didn't know till then that a total eclipse of the sun was happening. It was quite eerie as the moon slowly blocked out the sun. The light went, the birds stopped singing, the temperature dropped to 47 degrees and the street lighting came on! A car passed with dipped headlights and everything was silent. The sun's rays were too powerful to look at although I took some photographs shaded by the tree leaves. In places on the ground you could see crescent shapes on the ground, as the eclipse was reflected by the leaves. An hour later light returned, birds started to sing and the street lights went out.

I walked out of the town and stayed at the only Motel, for there was nowhere to camp or stay for another 25 miles.

ECLIPSE OF THE SUN

DAY 17—
INDEPENDENCE TO TROUTDALE—
25 miles (400 miles)

I felt refreshed, and set off along Highway 58 in high spirits towards Mouth of Wilson. The walking was enjoyable with rolling hills and the New River to cross. I began seeing wildlife—a bright yellow goldfinch flashed past, chipmunks squealed, groundhogs hurried away, and the hedgerows were full of flowers, particularly periwinkle and white campion. I knew I was well into mountains for the temperature never rose above 55 degrees. I called into the store at Mouth of Wilson and sat on a stool while I drank a couple of pints of milk and ate a king size packet of M & M's. The owner was full of praise for what I was doing and urged me to go via Troutdale to Damascus rather than follow Highway 58. She was right, for it turned out to be a magnificent walk.

First I headed up the hill to Troutdale and into Mount Rogers Recreation Area. Now I was close to the Appalachian Trail and Mount Rogers at 5,729 feet is the highest point in Virginia. I felt very strange being somewhere where I had actually walked through before. I called at the Post Office, and the owners son insisted on driving me to Marion where I could stay and make a radio broadcast in the morning. How I would get back to Troutdale I wasn't sure, but I decided something would happen. I felt quite pleased with myself; 400 miles now walked, and although tired after 25 miles, I was at last adjusting to my task.

THE APPALACHIANS

DAY 18— TROUTDALE TO DAMASCUS— 27 miles (427 miles)

In Marion I stayed at the Lincoln Hotel in the downtown area. In a country so geared to motels, it was strange to stay in a hotel, more the Britsh way of doing things, but you still had to go out and eat. A little after 7.0.a.m. I was through to BBC Radio Sheffield, live on the programme and chatted away about the walk for 8 minutes, instead of the usual three. I was beginning to wonder how I would get back to Troutdale when the hotel owner finally got through to the reporter at the Roanoake Times and Smyth County News. He would be delighted to take me in exchange for an interview. He insisted on showing me the area as we drove along the minor roads to Troutdale, stopping on the way to see Ripskin House, the home of a local author.

By 10a.m. I was finally walking along Highway 603, a small road weaving its way beneath Mt. Rogers. I knew I was in Appalachian Trail country and soon saw my first blaze and sign. I caressed it and let my mind float back to that walk. I had enjoyed it, although I found walking in trees day after day very oppressive. In the end I summed my feelings up in my log that night—'mixed feelings about the A.T.—so isolated on a tree path—much better my way with views, people and way of life.'

The road was little used and was really delightful walking past criss-cross pole fencing, so much a part of the Appalachain scene. There was pleasant woodland with dog wood in full bloom. Later I startled a couple of white tailed deer and saw my first pine marten. The temperature rose and as if confirming it was the first day of June it reached 70 degrees.

Beneath White Top mountain I regained Highway 58 at Konnarock and three hours later entered Damascus feeling tired and drained from the effort. I knew there was a place to stay for Appalachian Trail hikers but, partly because I was tired, I couldn't at first go there. I stopped at a diner and tucked into a huge meal and asked if they had a room. Fortunately the owner was out and instead of waiting,I fled to find the A.T. hostel. Just round the corner was the building boldly stating—'The Place—the Hilton of the A.T.' I went in feeling nervous but was soon made most welcome by the six occupants and rather over-awed them with my walk. It had taken them six weeks to walk the same mileage as I, who had only taken 18 days. They all craved for a beer and went out for one, but unashamedly I fell asleep.

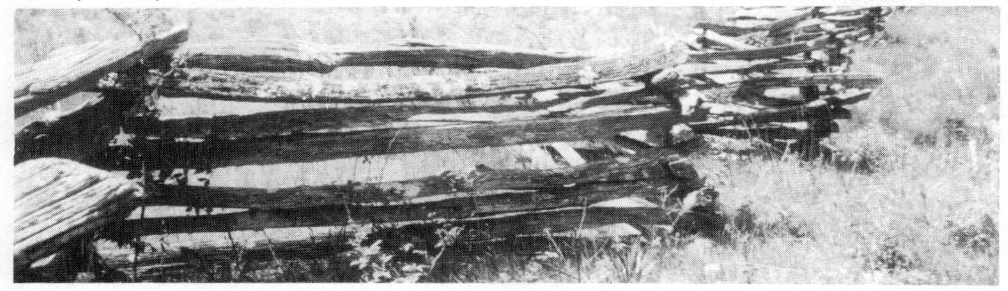

WOODEN FENCING

DAY 19—DAMASCUS TO BRISTOL—27 miles (454 miles)

I had hoped to sneak away quietly before anyone was awake but, just as I was about to leave, Tim Hogeboom appeared with cine camera in hand. The idea was that we would walk together for a couple of miles to a restaurant for breakfast, while he filmed me. He had set out from Springer Mountain in Georgia six weeks ago and planned not only to walk the 2,100 miles to Mt. Katahdin in Maine but to also make a film on the walk. I had a card from him at Christmas with his photo on the top of Mt. Katahdin; he reached there on October 10th, still with his cine camera.

Tim and I reached Clancy's Restaurant, only to find they served lunch and dinner and not breakfast! Tim was most upset for it was his idea and tab! But, like he wrote in his card, he still plans to buy me breakfast sometime. We bade farewell, he to continue up the trail and I along Highway 58 to Abingdon. There three hours later I ate a large breakfast. Refreshed, I hurried past the traffic for the Bristol Drag Racing event, since the schools were now closed for the summer and three months holiday, following Graduation Day.

Abingdon came as a pleasant surprise, with a population of 4,500, and full of interesting buildings. In 1768 it was known as Wolf Hill, after Daniel Boone had encountered wolves here on his way to Kentucky. Ten years later at the General Assembly it was renamed Abingdon. For me the attraction of the town was, by American standards, its old houses. The oldest, 'The Tavern' dates from 1779. The most impressive building is the Martha Washington Inn built in 1830 as the home of General Francis Preston. Opposite is Abingdon's chief attraction, the Barter Theatre, the oldest and longest running professional Equity theatre in America—from June 10th 1933. Many of the great actors have learnt their craft here, including Ernest Borgnine and Gregory Peck.

I pressed on along Highway 11 to Bristol. The temperature rose to 80 degrees, but I walked well. Even my feet seemed more comfortable and at last began to feel more normal. But I had made my mind up that the boots had to go and I would revert back to heavy traditional boots. I knew they would stand up to the task and give me no foot trouble. My next communication point was Mammoth Cave National Park, and I rang Sheila to send the boots there—two weeks walk to get there.To celebrate my well being I slipped into a Burger King and ate a Big Whopper!

GRAND GUITAR MUSIC MUSEUM

DAY 20—BRISTOL TO KINGSPORT— 24 miles (478 miles)

I was walking by 6.30a.m. after eating a Burger King breakfast. Three miles later and well into the down town area of Bristol, the City Editor, Ian Kemp, of the Bristol Herald, appeared to get my story and photograph. He was a keen jogger, and while I walked he jogged beside me, looking disgustingly fit. The road was lined with dog wood and three weeks earlier had looked stunning, with white and pink flowers, all beautifully manicured. After three miles Ian turned back to jog to his car.

As there seemed to be little facilities until Kingsport, I decided to walk along the two laned Highway 11W. The road proved quite enjoyable being through rolling wooded countryside, and not without incident. Two hours passed before a driver drove slowly past 'eyeing me'. I thought little of it until he came towards me ten minutes later. Being Sunday he was cruising around looking for a fellow male to play with. I thanked him for stopping and hurried on. He passed me again later but did not stop.

The roadside was busy with flea markets and yard sales. For about five miles I kept leap frogging a couple who were scouring the verges for aluminium cans. The back of their pick-up was full of a wide range of drink cans. Some people earn a living picking them up, for each can is worth a couple of cents.

The temperature reached almost 90 degrees for the first time for several days, and now just inside Tennessee State, on the fringe of Kingsport, I called it a day. My feet certainly felt better although my boots were already smooth on the soles. Reluctantly that night I threw my first pair of socks away.

THE PLACE, DAMASCUS

DAY 21—KINGSPORT TO DUFFIELD— 28 miles (506 miles)

I was away to get a few miles in before the heat began to slow me down. Infact it reached 87 degrees and I walked well despite it. First it was into Kingsport before joining Highway 23 and following it out of Tennessee back into Virginia to Duffield. Being Monday I hoped to get a copy of the Bristol Herald to see my story, and, at a Motel at the start of Highway 23, picked up a copy and saw my face on the front cover! Not long afterwards a car pulled up and the driver shook me by the hand and wished me luck. He had seen me walking for the last three days as he travelled to work and wondered what I was up to.

The highway, although two-laned, was exciting to walk along, being cut through the hills. At the bottom of one hill was an old gas station where I purchased a couple of pints of milk to spur me on the final few miles. A little further on my right was Natural Tunnel State Park, a natural limestone tunnel 850 feet long and 10 stories high. Through it runs a railroad part of the Early Historical Railroad Museum. Unfortunately it was four miles in the opposite direction so I pressed on, being overtaken by a train half a mile long.

Close to Duffield I turned left, west, again opposite the monument to Daniel Boone. Here I began to follow the line of the Wilderness Road that he cut in 1775, through Cumberland Gap into Kentucky. Daniel Boone was born in Pennsylvania in 1734. He became a noted hunter and in 1767 set off to explore the west and in 1775 had set up home in Boonesville in Kentucky.I decided to celebrate and stayed at the Ramada Inn—there was no where else anyway—and had a swim and a glass of California rose wine to record walking over 500 miles.

STORE AND OWNER

DAY 22—DUFFIELD TO JONESVILLE—22 miles (528 miles)

Thick mist covered the area as I set off on Highway 58 as it ascended Powell Mountain. Being cool, the walking was pleasant, but did not last for long; by 9.0 a.m. it was 80 degrees. It was good to be back on a small road again with little traffic. At frequent intervals I came to historical markers. One on Warren Ridge recorded where Daniel Boone's son had been killed. Later in the valley another told of an Indian massacre in June 1785 when the notorious half breed, Benge, killed the family of Archibald Scott, the husband and five children. His wife was captured but later escaped.

In the early afternoon I entered Jonesville, having been walking for eight hours and only drank four pints of milk. Jonesville was founded in 1794 after Frederick Jones and the County seat of Lee, my last county in Virginia. I called at the Post Office to mail some film back to Britain for processing. I caused quite a stir when I mentioned what I was doing, and at the local motel was given twenty postcards, to 'write to the folks back home.'

JONESVILLE SIGN

JONESVILLE HISTORICAL MARKER

DAY 23—JONESVILLE TO WILDERNESS ROAD CAMPGROUND (CUMBERLAND GAP NATIONAL HISTORICAL PARK)— 35 MILES (563 miles)

I was off again early, before 7.0a.m., but the temperature soon topped 90 degrees. I never intended to walk so far this day, but perhaps it was a fitting end to Virginia, pushing myself hard for the Pacific. Leaving Jonesville I passed the marker to Doctor Stills. He was born nearby in 1828 and is the founder of Osteopathy. A little later I was amazed to see an American ploughing by hand. In such a mechanised and wealthy country, one assumes everyone is well off; we waved to each other.

First I headed for Rose Hill before Ewing. All the time now the mountains were drawing closer on either side, funnelling me towards the gap. After Rose Hill, a telephone maintainance van stopped and offered me ice cold water, it was like nectar. Opposite us was an Indian burial mound, while flanking the hill were the renowned White Rocks, a familar landmark on the Wilderness Road. Close by was a Colonial Fort, built in 1768 of half a dozen cabins surrounded by a strong stockade. Frequent harassment by Indians forced them to abandon it.

At Ewing I was two thirds of the way to the campground, and stopped to have a hamburger to build up my energy to get there. While eating, the reporter from the Middlesborough paper—the Daily News—in Kentucky caught up with me. He photographed me outside, striding along. Next day I was on the front page—'fueled by ambition, takes hike in his stride.'

I knew I must simply keep going or I would feel tired and want to stop. I was determined to get there and, close to the entrance to the Historical Park, called at the gas station for a couple of pints of milk to give me the final impetus. A mile later I reached the campsite sign, only to discover the campsite was more than a mile away. After exactly 12 hours of walking doing 35 miles, I reached the startled Ranger's office. Amazed at what I was doing they insisted on being photographed with me and still charged me $5 to camp! There were more than 250 sites but only three campers; I was the only one in a tent. Just after the tent was up a Ranger called round saying, 'he thought I would like some fruit'—a large bagfull. After eating fifteen apples, I gave up and did not eat another apple for two weeks.

Tomorrow I would cross the gap and enter my second State, Kentucky. I slept solidly.

WHITE ROCKS; CUMBERLAND GAP NATIONAL HISTORICAL PARK

KENTUCKY—THE VOLUNTEER STATE
The Commonwealth of Kentucky—
'United We Stand, Divided We Fall'.

CAPITAL—FRANKFORT

POPULATION (1970 CENSUS)—3,219,311

HIGHEST ELEVATION— BLACK MOUNTAIN PEAK, 4,150 FEET.

LOWEST ELEVATION—MISSISSIPPI RIVER, IN FULTON COUNTY, 257 FEET.

TOTAL AREA—40,395 SQUARE MILES.

The 25th state admitted to the Union in 1792, and the first west of the mountains. Renowned for its tobacco, Bluegrass, horses, whisky (bourbon) and fried chicken! State bird—cardinal—about 300 different species have been sighted in Kentucky.

JOHN MERRILL AND RANGERS

KENTUCKY

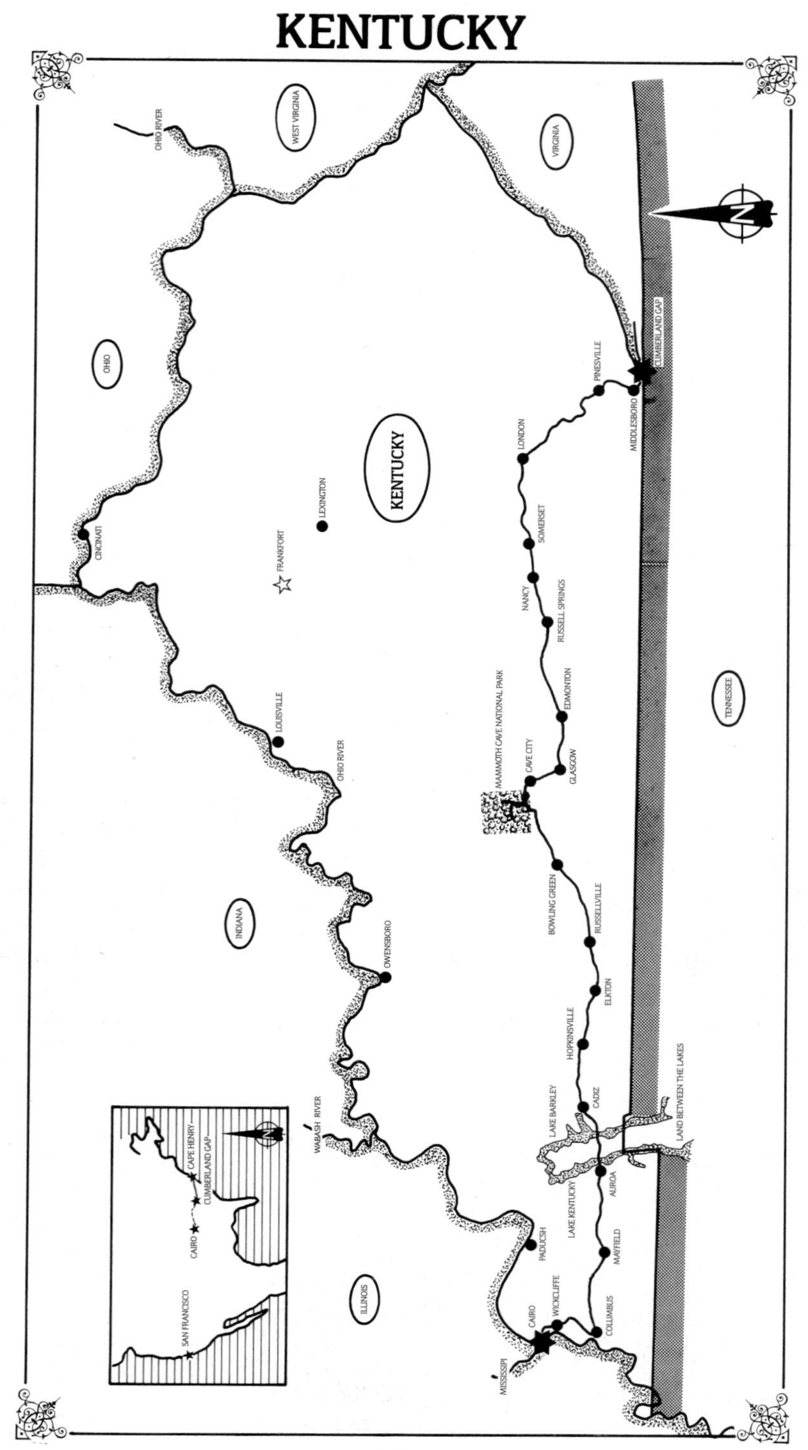

OHIO RIVER
WEST VIRGINIA
VIRGINIA
OHIO
KENTUCKY
LEXINGTON
FRANKFORT
CINCINATI
CUMBERLAND GAP
PINESVILLE
MIDDLESBORO
LONDON
SOMERSET
NANCY
RUSSELL SPRINGS
EDMONTON
MAMMOTH CAVE NATIONAL PARK
CAVE CITY
GLASGOW
TENNESSEE
LOUISVILLE
OHIO RIVER
INDIANA
OWENSBORO
BOWLING GREEN
RUSSELLVILLE
ELKTON
HOPKINSVILLE
CADIZ
LAKE BARKLEY
LAND BETWEEN THE LAKES
WABASH RIVER
LAKE KENTUCKY
AUROA
MAYFIELD
PADUCSH
ILLINOIS
WICKCLIFFE
CAIRO
COLUMBUS
MISSISIPI
CAPE HENRY
CUMBERLAND GAP
CAIRO
SAN FRANCISCO

DAY 24—WILDERNESS ROAD CAMPGROUND TO PINEVILLE— 20 MILES (583 MILES).

I left early to ascend the road to the summit of Cumberland Gap and enter Kentucky. The battered state sign said welcome and displayed a race horse. The traffic raced by oblivious to the historical significance of the Gap. I descended the hill racing towards the Visitor's Centre, my first communication point. I always looked forward to news and letters from Sheila, but was quite crestfallen when none had arrived, only my maps for Kentucky.

Cumberland Gap Historical Park was formed in 1943 and is the second largest one in America. The Gap is a natural break in the Cumberland Mountains and is 800 feet deep. Before Daniel Boone came and cut his way through, the Gap was known and formed part of an ancient Indian Trail. The Wilderness Road was the first gateway to the west and within 25 years of it opening, more than 300,000 people had passed through.

I was feeling hungry and slightly upset at no letters. I pressed on into Middlesborough for a late breakfast. I was also feeling tired from the big effort I had made the previous day.The town has strong English ties and was last century a model Britsh Town, with one of the oldest golf courses in America. I looked at the streets full of tempting signs—motels and eating houses. But it was too early to stop—only 10.30 a.m.! I decided to head northwards along Highway 25E towards Pinesville and onto London. There was little alternative as nothing headed westwards without detouring around.

I set off along the road after purchasing the Middlesborough paper and seeing my photograph and story. The road was busy and hot and I ambled along and kept looking back at Middlesborough, wondering if I should have stopped. The 13 miles to Pineville sapped me as the temperature topped 90 degrees and the humidity was high. I debated about camping at Pine Mountain State Resort Park, but was out of the way. I also had to do another radio progress report in the morning, so I decided to find a motel. After seeing the clean and attractive Middlesborough, Pinesville came as a shock, being dirty and uninteresting. In fact it was one of the worst places I stayed at. I found the only motel beside the road and checked in before ringing Sheila and letting her know, I had had no letters and was now in Kentucky.

KENTUCKY STATE SIGN

DAY 25—PINESVILLE TO BARBOURVILLE—21 MILES (604 MILES)

I was off just after 6.0a.m. first to find a restaurant for breakfast before contacting BBC Radio Sheffield. I found a restaurant but no phone. In the end I used theirs in the kitchen and spoke on the air for ten minutes, with cooking sound effects! The sun soon broke through and again topped 91 degrees. I wrote in my log that night, 'the 3 H's again—hot humid and horrible!'.

I continued along Highway 25E and stopped at Flat Lick to post my Virginia maps and information back to Britain. Flat Lick was at first an Indian Camp, later a Long Hunters' Camp. In 1769 Daniel Boone was here and three historic routes—Boone's Trace to Boonesborough; the Wilderness Road to Crab Orchard and the Warrior's Path to the mouth of the Scioto River—converge here to join and travel to Cumberland Gap.

The Post Master had read about me in the paper and quickly gave me a mug of coffee. A local walked in and recognised me and insisted on the paying the postage! I thanked her profusely and thought life wasn't so bad after all. Three miles later I stopped at a Trading Post for some milk and was again recognised and given a quart free.

8 miles later I passed a motel and wondered whether to stop, but pressed on wondering if I would find something else. I decided to try in Barbourville and stayed in the College Motel, opposite Union College. The town was very attractive and everyone most helpful. I felt in such good spirits, I washed my clothes; something I rarely do on a walk! I looked at my T shirt; it was badly stained and smelt terrible. It would have to go and I surprised myself by throwing it away. I bought a new one and wore it for the next five months to San Francisco! I purchased new insoles for my boots before going out to celebrate, with a hamburger from a Sonic Drive-in.

PINESVILLE

DAY 26—BARBOURVILLE TO LONDON—27 MILES (631 MILES)

Couldn't find anywhere for breakfast, so went without and was walking just after dawn at 6.15a.m. Dusk was at 9.0p.m. Again hot, into the early 90's. I regained Highway 25E and continued along it to Bailey's Switch. Here I turned right onto Highway 229, a small road, which proved a more direct way to London, through pleasant peaceful countryside and still following the line of the Wilderness Road.

The countryside was mostly farming, with young corn in the fields and fields with a few horses. At Laurel Fork I was feeling extremely hungry and called into the village store for milk and a sandwich. The owner was a 29 year old who read the bible all day. He was a true bible thumping evangelist who quoted from memory many passages to back up his discussion points. He envied my walk to be alone with the wilds and meeting allsorts of people from different walks of life. He too would have liked to undertake my journey to see the wonders of God. I could only agree with his points although I could identify the closeness of God to me and how he 'helped me' along the way.

Opposite was Camp Ground Methodist Church, the building dating from 1876. In 1790 it was made from logs and was a popular place on the Wilderness Road. A little further up the road I came to the site of the Wilderness Inn, which was built in 1804 but caught fire in 1962. Two miles later I passed Levi Jackson State Park and was tempted to stop, first to swim in the pool, camp and explore a preserved section of the Wilderness Road. But I was a little tired and intrigued to see London, for I was born in London, England. Four miles later I entered the town with a population 4,002 on the sign. I was rather like a child seeing the London Post Office, and couldn't resist staying at the London Mall Motel.

Having only eaten a sandwich all day I went to a nearby restaurant which was beautifully decorated in Victorian style. It never ceased to amaze me that where ever I went, I was readily accepted wearing just a T shirt and shorts. I ordered a rib-eye steak and noticed on the menu, frog's legs. I had heard them croaking on the ponds beside the Wilderness Road. Eaten I felt better, and began to appreciate that I was getting fitter and my feet were not causing any problem, and I was losing weight. I put my feet up and watched T.V. seeing Swale win the Belmont Stakes earlier the day. The motel owner gave me a mileage card—direct, San Francisco was 2,480 miles—it didn't seem far!

ENTERING LONDON

DAY 27—LONDON TO SOMERSET—27 MILES (666 MILES)

From London, I left the Wildnerness Road and began heading west once more along Highway 80. On the way through London, I saw the historical marker to the Battle of London. On August 17th 1862, a Confederate cavalry attacked American troops, killing 13, wounding 17, and capturing 111 men and 40 wagons. The rest escaped over the Cumberland Gap. English place names continued to scatter the area, with Somerset the end of the day's walk, Lake Cumberland not far away, Manchester lay to the east and Glasgow was five days away.

Highway 80 cut its way through the Daniel Boone National Forest and was a magnificent undulating walk past trees, gorges and deep rivers. The forest runs almost from the Ohio border to Tennessee and covers 1,500,000 acres. In it are some spectacular scenery, but for me awkward to get to without backtracking a lot. A pity for the pictures of Laurel River Lake and Cumberland Falls looked very impressive.

As the day wore on the temperature topped 95 and I went 26 miles before getting a can of orange from a closed gas station. Being Sunday many places were closed and luckily I had a couple of quarters for the slot machine. Three miles later I reached an open gas station with a store and surprised them by buying half a gallon of milk and drinking the lot. I felt much better and pressed on. There was nowhere to camp or stay and I simply walked along the highway; now a dual-laned one.

I knew I was pushing it, and after 12 hours of continuous walking on milk and an orange drink, reached Somerset after 35 miles. I stayed in the first motel that I came to and surprised myself by having a swim in the pool for twenty minutes. I was obviously on a 'high' despite the day's effort. I drank several cokes before walking down to 'Long John Silvers' for a seafood salad. I knew I was also tired for I had push myself to find somewhere to eat. My thirst still remained unquenched and on the way back to the motel I called into a store for a few packets of M & M's and a pint of strawberry ice-cream. In my room I lay on the bed watching T.V. and ate all the ice cream and candy!

HIGHWAY 80

DAY 28—
SOMERSET TO RUSSELL SPRINGS—
28 MILES (692 MILES)

I reluctantly set off walking at 7.0a.m. for the effect of yesterday's long day had not worn off, despite ten hours of sleep. I had hoped to walk along the Cumberland Parkway but pedestrians are banned and I had to follow Highway 80 which went to the same places but was considerably longer. First I headed south and across a spur of Lake Cumberland. The lake covers an area of more than 50,000 acres and has a shoreline of 1,200 miles—the length of the south coast of England, from London to Land's End.

Beyond I reached Nancy feeling lethargic. I posted more film back from here before reaching Windsor, three hours and nine miles later. Here I downed another half gallon of milk for energy, but felt tired instead. I headed on to the Russell County Line and my first time zone—Central Standard Time. I was now another hour behind Britain, but could not grasp the fact. A mile later I sat beside the road and when a car pulled up and offered to take me to a motel in Russell Springs, five miles away, I hadn't the heart to refuse.

LAKE CUMBERLAND

DAY 29—RUSSELL SPRINGS TO COLUMBIA—22 MILES (714 MILES)

The Postman gave me a lift back to the County line and Central Time Zone sign. I placed the rucksack thirty feet from the sign and balanced the camera on top. Using the 8 second delayed timer I had sufficent time to run back to sign, smile and look happy before hearing the click! This was the only way to get photographs of myself at key places along the route. I took three photographs to make sure. When I look at them now, I am quite jealous of the beautiful tan I had! Anyone seeing me running back and forwards would have wondered at my sanity.

Two hours of walking brought me to Russell Springs where I had slept. I called in at Hardee's for breakfast—English muffins - something we don't have in Britain! An hour later I was back on Highway 80 heading first of all to Royville and then onto Columbia, the county seat of Adair, established in 1801.

I was glad to have an 'easier' day for I was still feeling lethargic, but I suspected the heat was upsetting me unknowingly. This was the fifth day the temperature was in the early 90's. Apparently this was very unusual, more like August instead of being early June. The cause was a Bermuda high. I was now three days behind my original schedule but had walked 714 miles, as against 701 miles on paper. The reason lay in the road maps; they do not give the mileage through the cities, only to the city limits, which entailed further walking. However, I was not unduly worried. I was well on my way, through my first State and now my first time zone.

JOHN MERRILL AND CENTRAL TIME ZONE

DAY 30—COLUMBIA TO EDMONTON—24 MILES (738 MILES)

Although I had passed through into Standard Time, I could not adjust my watch, and put it back an hour. For three days I could not accept the fact that I was basically in the same area, but now a further hour behind Britain. Eventually, I did adjust it but for the moment I left it.

Again it was hot and there was little change for the next five days—90 degrees plus each day was forecast. I was not the only one suffering, the fields were full of tobacco plants and should have been quite large by this time. Instead they were small and dying in the fields. Everyone was upset as the previous year, 1983, had also been hot and a drought forced many into liquidation.

The walking was pleasant through rolling countryside but the heat made me suffer. I walked 20 miles before getting a drink and something to eat. That night I learnt the temperature reached 96 degrees, 'no wonder I felt strange.' I was glad to reach Edmonton and stay in an air conditioned motel—Cave Hill Motel. Very friendly and helpful people and only charged me $10 to stay. At night the temperature only dropped to 70 degrees.

TOBACCO FIELD

DAY 31—EDMONTON TO CAVE CITY—20 MILES (758 MILES)

I was walking early in an effort to 'beat the heat' for a while, but it was soon topping 90 degrees. I was sorry to leave Edmonton with its unspoilt and attractive square, friendly people, the cheapest motel I have stayed in and an interested local reporter. I set off along Highway 80 heading for Glasgow 15 miles away. The city was established in 1799 and is the seat of Barren County. I photographed many of Glasgow's key places, such as the Post Office, High School and airport. Mostly because my wife would have been amused, for she lived for many years close to Glasgow in Scotland, which has a population of 816,000; Glasgow, Kentucky is 15,000!

I was now into 'Cave Country' and turned right onto Highway 90, heading directly for Mammoth Cave National Park, my first National Park. I was quite excited but knew I couldn't walk there in a day and nearing Cave City stopped, leaving about the same distance to walk the next day into the park. The rolling countryside was about 700 feet above sea level, and the fields full of sunburnt shrivelled tobacco plants. I didn't seem to be making much headway westwards, San Francisco was 2,420 miles away; five days ago it was 2,480 and I had walked 127 miles from there!

GLASGOW HIGH SCHOOL

DAY 32—CAVE CITY TO MAMMOTH CAVE NATIONAL PARK CAMPGROUND—24 MILES (782 MILES)

Before leaving I rang both my local radio stations, BBC Radio Sheffield and Derby to give a progress report, live on the air. I set off in high spirits and plunged into tourist land, with motels galore and all the favourite eating places, Wendy's, Pizza Hut, MacDonalds, steak houses and a Jellystone campground and water slide. As my guidebook said, 'Cave City has the highest concentration of commercial attractions in the immediate vicinity of Mammoth Cave.'

After devouring a Wendy's hamburger, I hurried on into the National Park. The thought of letters, new boots and trails to follow, gave me an almost heady existence. I came the back way into the park, as this appeared the shortest route. It was certainly quiet and through extensive woodland, en route passing the site of Sand Cave. Floyd Collins was the first to explore the cave in 1925 but became trapped when fallen rock blocked a passage. The rescue attempt lasted several days, but further rock falls ended his life.

Entering the main visitor's area I headed for the Post Office and was delighted to get my new sturdy boots, but no letters. I put the tent up but was quite excited to have reached my first National Park. I checked to see when you could go down the cave system but I was too late. I laced my new boots on (they had been broken in ready) and followed a trail to Green River. I literally skipped along, glad to be on a trail and with no pack to carry. I reached the river just in time to get on the Miss Green River boat. I sat at the bow with my feet up as we glided gently along the definitely green coloured river. We saw wood duck and chicks, white tailed deer and a fawn, jays, woodpeckers and a stunningly red bird which I assumed must be a cardinal. As we docked a large three foot snake swam across the river.

I ran back to the tent, delighted to have a sturdy pair of boots on. To celebrate getting here I ate out in the lodge, after watching a racoon nosey around for food in the wood nearby. To complete the day I rang Sheila to tell her the boots had arrived and the old worn out pair were now on their way back as a souvenir. After writing my log, my final act of the day was to finally put my watch back an hour and be on Standard Time.

MISS GREEN RIVER 11

DAY 33—MAMMOTH CAVE TO PARK CITY—15 MILES (797 MILES)

There are more than 2,000 caves in Kentucky and the State is often referred to as the cave capital of the U.S.A. Mammoth Cave is by far the largest; in fact, at just over 200 miles long, it is the longest cave system in the world. The cave has been known about for at least 4,500 years and early Indians used blazing torches to search for minerals. The cave was formed 300 million years ago when a shallow inland sea covered the area. Subterranean water dissolved the porous rock and as it receded left dry passageways.The cave was 'officially' discovered in 1799 and during the War of 1812 miners used oil lamps to mine nitrates used in the manufacture of gunpowder. Two years later a hotel was operating close to the cave's entrance.

The National Park covers an area of 52,000 acres; mostly hardwood forest. There are only 34 miles of trails and the park is within a day's drive of 100,000,000 people! There are several tours both above and below ground and I decided to take the 'very strenuous, 4 mile, 4½ hour tour' through a section of the cave. I joined about 200 people and we began our descent into the truly mammoth cave. Inside it was a constant 54°F (12°C) with humidity of 87%. I enjoyed the coolness after the recent 90 degrees of heat.

The walk was full of variety, sometimes along massive tunnels with high ceilings and others through smaller passageways, such as Fat Man's Misery. Approximately halfway we stopped at the Snowball dining room. The gypsum-clustered ceilings are just like snowballs. The room is huge with tables and chairs and it was most strange to get hot food and ice cold coke, 267 feet below ground. Apart from the spectacular domes, caverns and pits, the masterpiece of the walk was to see the Frozen Niagrara. A huge display of stalactites and stalagmites. Coming out into the fresh and hot air made you sweat immediately.

I was reluctant to leave but felt I must continue my trek westwards, and by early afternoon the rucksack was strapped onto my back again and I set off snail-like to Park City. I assumed it would be similar to Cave City, full of amenities. I passed a KOA campground on the way and wavered but decided to get a few more miles under my belt. When I reached Cave City there was nothing! I couldn't believe it. I was told there was a motel nearby on Highway 31W, on my route. I hurried on in the now early evening and came to fields and no motel. By 8.0p.m. I began to feel a bit depressed and suddenly saw a Best Western sign. I ascended the half mile long drive and reached a splendid resort. I felt distinctly out of place, but was made very welcome. I don't think a bearded backpacker had ever stopped before.

I was now really adjusting to my task. The boots seemed fine and I enjoyed Kentucky's scenery. Like their slogan—Oh! Kentucky—you'll come to love it—I was falling under its spell. For the first time since setting off, I wrote postcards to a few friends and a long joyful letter to Sheila.

WORN OUT FIRST PAIR OF BOOTS

DAY 34—PARK CITY TO BOWLING GREEN—24 MILES (821 MILES)

I was late setting off, mostly because I could not tear myself away from the extensive breakfast spread! By 8.0a.m. I was back on Highway 31W heading for Bowling Green. Around me was attractive farmland and a limestone ridge on my right. After four hours of walking the road became dual carriageway, and seeing a Mini Mart I stopped for a drink and a cool down in the shade—over 90 degrees again!

I sat in a quiet corner of the store making my drink last as long as possible, even munching the ice cubes! Just about to leave and continue along the road when a cyclist, Ron Grossman, joined me. It proved a momentous chance meeting—he was cycling from coast to coast! He had set off twelve days before and planned to reach the Pacific in about five weeks. I am afraid that I bored the pants off him as I told Ron about the walk. I was sorry to see him go. When I returned to Britain five months later, I saw the card he had sent my wife from Cairo in Illinois state. Ron wrote to Sheila saying, 'he was in good spirits.... I think of your husband as very humble but steadfast in purpose. Meeting him is inspirational, to my own travels.' Ron was the only person I met doing a major undertaking as I walked across the U.S.A.

I continued on along the highway, limping slightly as a blister began to develop on my left heel—'back to square one with boots!'. An hour later I entered Bowling Green. I decided on a motel; there was a campground at Beech Bend Park, a little off my route, but the thought of camping on one of the largest campgrounds in the world, with 6,500 sites, just did not appeal.

Bowling Green was founded in 1798 at the stopping point of west- bound settlers at Big Spring. Here Robin Moore turned his cabin into an inn and for his guests' entertainment had a bowling green. The game was popular in New York along the Hudson River at this time. Carved wooden balls were rolled across the grass; hence the city's name. Since then Bowling Green has grown into Kentucky's fifth largest city with a population of 47,990. Perhaps its best known industry is General Motors plant, where the original American sportscar, the Corvette, is made. Fifteen cars an hour come off the assembly line. As I walked I often fantasised about what car I should like to drive. Depending on my mood it was either a Corvette or Trans-Am; other times any four by four would do, such as a Jeep or Renegrade, later I decided to settle for a chauffer driven Cadillac!

MARIAN MOORE HOUSE, BOWLING GREEN

DAY 35—BOWLING GREEN TO AUBURN—22 MILES (843 MILES)

My route through Bowling Green proved historical, setting the theme of the day. First I passed Mariah Moore House, now a restaurant, but was built by Robert Moore in the late 18th century, and named after his daughter. The building has been restored and is the oldest brick home in Bowling Green. Close by was Fountain Square, on the site of the famous bowling green. The ascent up the hill past very attractive houses brought me to the campus of the Western Kentucky University, with its many noble buildings, extensive lawns and sports complex.

Leaving the city behind, I followed Highway 68. The heat was already affecting me. At 7.0 a.m. it was 84°F and two hours later 94°F. My face soon became burnt and my pace slowed, and I walked listlessly along. After a couple of hours I stopped for refreshment and was given a free hamburger and a couple of cokes. Feeling refreshed I walked on to South Union and Shakertown.

I knew nothing of this religious group and, having spent several years at a Quaker school, I was intrigued to learn more. I walked into the main building and was made most welcome, and on learning about my walk there was nothing to pay. Shakers were founded in America by Ann Lee, a former Quaker, in 1776. There were several Shaker communities, all were 'believers in Christ's Second Appearing.' The property was common to all, celibacy was the rule once you joined the community, whether married or not, and you lived like brother and sister. The Centre House that I was in dates from 1824 and has a divided staircase—one side for women, the other for men.

The term Shaker derives from their religious worship, when they dance around the room singing a hymn and clapping their hands. The South Union Society began in 1807 and at its height in 1827 had 349 members. Almost a century later in 1922 there were only seven and everything was auctioned. Originally their land covered 6,000 acres with 200 buildings. They were renowned for their hard work, good food and hospitality. Many travellers stopped such as President James Munroe and General Andrew Jackson. They were always at the forefront of the latest equipment, with water piped into their kitchens in the 1830's, and by early 1900 had bathrooms and telephones. They made all their own furniture and a considerable amount was on display.

I was sorry to leave but glad of the rest, especially as both my heels were sore. All part of the readjustment to a new pair of boots, but I was happy about the way my feet were settling down. I presed on to Auburn and stayed there.

SHAKER BUILDING

DAY 36—AUBURN TO ELKTON—26 MILES (869 MILES)

The heat was definitly sapping my strength and it reached the mid 90's again. I left at 6.0a.m. to walk as much as possible before the heat made me listless. I followed Highway 80/68 to Russellville and seat of Logan County. Historically the town is interesting, with the homes of three Kentucky Governors, and the Old Southern Bank building on 6th and Main, built in 1810, was the scene in 1868 of a holdup by Jesse James' gang. They wounded the Bank President and escaped with $9,000.

Nearby was a historical marker to Col. James Bowie, born in Logan county, a famed Texas ranger and co-commander of The Alamo. There with 187 others they chose death rather than surrender. The battle cry of the Texas victory of 1836 was 'Remember the Alamo.' Bowie designed the famous bowie knife, used extensively in the frontier days and now.

I pressed on to Elkton 16 miles away passing a huge model bull beside the road, saying 'Nelson Cole, Quality Used Cars, and that's no bull!' Later Major's welding shop, which looked deserted and just had a collapsed pickup with hood and front on the floor. I was definitely walking better and my feet were settling down to the new boots, with my blisters now hardening off.

Entering Elkton, I felt extremely thirsty having drunk nothing all day. Nearing the downtown area a friendly local offered me a jar of ice cold water. I sat down and drank three pints of it. My friend was the local police officer just come off duty, with a revolver in his back pocket. He advised me, like everyone else, had up to now, that I should not camp on my own beside the road.Asked if there was any trouble here—'Not now', he said, 'I've locked them all up!' A little later the District Attorney called and wished me luck. Feeling in safe hands I went into the town for a meal and a place to stay. That evening a violent storm passed through, bending trees and dropping 1½ inches of rain. An hour later the sun was shining!

NELSON COLE—USED CARS

DAY 37—ELKTON TO HOPKINSVILLE—22 MILES (891 MILES)

Left early—'heat beating'—along Highway 68 to Fairview for breakfast at the store, of sugar coated cakes and a pint of milk. Opposite was the obelisk—351 feet high and the fourth highest in the US—to Jefferson Davis. He was born here in 1808 and went on to become a Senator and later Secretary for War under President Pierce. In 1861 he became the first and only President of the Confederate States of America—1861-65. I had hoped to take the elevator to the top to view the surrounding area but I was too early.

I pressed on to Hopkinsville, a large city with a population of 30,000, established in 1797. My money supply was getting low. I had decided not to carry a lot of money, preferring to use my credit cards and my American Express gold card to get money. I was down to $100 and called into a bank in Hopkinsville for money. Whilst Americans can get money from a Bank with a gold card, a foreigner can't. I would have to call at an American Express office. The nearest was in Missouri; I would have to manage.

Still hot into the 90's but the weather looked as though it was breaking up, with another storm and deluge in mid afternoon. I was glad I was in a motel, for in a tent I would have floated away. I photographed the downpour with the water overflowing the guttering and shooting jets of water high into the air.The roads were flooded within ten minutes.The next day was the first day of official summer—June 21st!

JEFFERSON MONUMENT

DAY 38—HOPKINSVILLE TO CADIZ—22 MILES (913 MILES)

The storm had certainly cooled everything down and it was very pleasant to be walking in cooler temperatures, although later it did reach 90 degrees, for the fourteenth day in a row. Today was also the first day of summer and the longest day. I followed Highway 68, first to Gracey where the Post Office gave me an ice cold coke, and then onto Cadiz. On the way I passed a large herd of cattle wallowing in a pool of water and a huge Marlboro country sign, complete with larger than life size cowboy. I wanted to walk further but there was nothing ahead.

Cadiz is the gateway to the Land Between the Lakes country, and I called at the tourist office for information on the area and to check whether the ferry across the Mississippi River at Columbus was running. I collected some leaflets and was informed the ferry was operating everyday, between 6.0a.m. and 6.0p.m. How wrong they proved to be!

I was now five days behind my original schedule, but had walked an extra 120 miles to this point. I wasn't worried, I felt fine, settling down well and my boots were proving comfortable and supportive. Even the rucksack seemed lighter! My only regret was that I did not have enough time to make detours to see more fully Lake Barkley and the Land Between the lakes I would cross the next day.

MARLBORO SIGN BOARD

DAY 39—CADIZ TO AURORA—22 MILES (935)

The Land Between the Lakes is a huge project of the Tennessee Valley Authority. Situated between two massive lakes—Lake Barkley and Kentucky Lake—is a wooded peninsula of land approximately 8 miles wide and 40 miles long—170, 000 acres. It is a major outdoor area with many sorts of activities and numerous campsites. The area is scenically very attractive and a joy to walk through. I followed Highway 68 through Canton to Lake Barkley and its mile-long bridge. The lake is the second biggest in Kentucky—118 miles long with a shoreline of over 1,000 miles—more than Wales in Britain!

Across and onto the forest of Land Between the Lakes. The weather was hot and sticky—90 degrees again—but the clouds looked ominous and near the Golden Pond historical marker, a storm moved in for half an hour. I wondered if this was the site where the famous film—On Golden Pond—starring Henry and Jane Fonda—was based but no one seemed to know. There was a town here between 1882-1969 and the pond is named after the golden reflection of the sunrays on the pond. A little further I came to the Visitor's Centre turn-off. I followed it but became annoyed when it was so geared to cars and meant walking back on myself, that I gave up in disgust.

Kentucky Lake was colossal, being 2½ times bigger than Lake Barkley. Being 134 miles with a surface area of 160,000 acres, it has a shoreline of 2,380 miles—almost the coastline of Scotland! I crossed the road bridge to Aurora, named after the Greek goddess of the dawn. Although it was only early afternoon, I stopped early, as though guided. Had I carried on I might not have lived to tell the tale.

LAKE BARKLEY BRIDGE

DAY 40—AURORA TO MAYFIELD—30 MILES (965 MILES)

The previous night I looked at the map and decided to push myself and reach the Mississippi River in two days' time. I knew it would mean walking 30 miles both days, but I could not resist the challenge. I went without breakfast and was walking by 5.45a.m. I continued on along Highway 80 towards Hardin. After three miles I reached a devastated area, with snapped and uprooted trees and demolished mobile homes. Had I continued walking from Aurora the previous day, I would have reached here at 3.0p.m. the exact time that a tornado passed through, causing havoc. On my right were two mobile homes. One was unscathed, the other totally demolished. The owner sat on the twisted remains, waiting for the insurance man to call! I photographed the sad sight.

Opposite was another house with a three foot thick tree beside it. The tornado had come past uprooted the tree and left the house untouched! A few yards down the road and you could see the path of the tornado through the trees, with smashed trees on either side. I pressed onto Hardin 6 miles away for a late breakfast of hash browns, two eggs over-easy and several cups of coffee. During breakfast the weather dramatically changed and, on leaving the restaurant, the sky was pitch black and the wind had whipped up. 'Better sit this out', I thought and went into a barber's shop for a hair cut. Something I rarely do on a walk, but on hearing my story the barber cut my hair and beard free! Outside it lashed with rain, the street lights came on and the traffic lights swayed alarmingly in the gusty wind. Fifteen minutes later the sun came out and I continued on.

Two miles later I sheltered in a barn as another storm passed through, the last of the day. For the first time for two weeks the temperature did not reach 90 degrees, only 87. I followed the quiet Highway 80 to Brewers and towards Mayfield. Approaching there in the late afternoon I stopped at a hamburger stand—Jack King's Drive In—and was given a huge meal free by the owner. He wanted me to stay for a couple of days and rest but couldn't understand my driving ambition. I knew I was pushing it and had already developed a small blister on my right heel, but my mind was made up and I reached Mayfield an hour later, rather tired.

TORNADO DAMAGE

DAY 41—MAYFIELD TO COLUMBUS—31 MILES (996 MILES)

Refreshed, I walked a mile to breakfast before following the final segment of Highway 80 to Columbus and the Mississippi River. It was the thought of getting to the great river, to see my third state and to have walked my 1,000 miles, that sustained me as I walked. I knew I was overdoing it, for my feet felt sore all over. This was really my own fault since I had not washed any socks recently or bought any new ones.

There was no need to push so hard but I simply kept walking, first through the attractive village of Fancy Farm and onto Milburn and Arlington. Here at 'Trail's End', I rested while eating a hamburger. I walked on wearily now and two hours later entered Columbus. To celebrate I purchased the ingredients for a tuna salad, half a gallon of milk, and a pair of socks. The final mile brought me to Columbus-Belmont Battlefield State Park, where I camped close to a confederate trench.

The camp owner was shocked at my blistered and cut feet but I was happy to be here. From my tent I gazed across the Mississippi and watched quarter of a mile long barges slowly ascending the river. I enquired about the ferry and was devastated to learn it wasn't operating. In fact it had not been working for three years! So much for the assurance given at the Tourist Office at Cadiz. I decided I would have to walk northwards and cross the road bridge to Cairo in Illinois state, before crossing the Mississippi to Missouri.

For the moment I sat overlooking the wide majestic river slowly consuming my half gallon of milk. A shower soon revived me further and I put new socks on my battered feet. Close to the campsite is a museum displaying items from the Civil War and an anchor and chain intended to stop the Union boats. The museum's building was formerly a Civil War infirmary. I needed no rocking that night.

COLUMBUS CAMP

DAY 42—COLUMBUS TO OHIO (ILLINOIS)—29 MILES (1,025 MILES)

It has never ceased to amaze me how, on every walk that I do, my feet return to normal after a few hours rest and my blisters dry up. Although I may be tired the night before, in the morning I am raring to go and full of vigour. I was walking by 6.15a.m. and followed Highway 123 northwards to Bardwell. Here I joined Highway 62/51 for Wickliffe and the Ohio River.

On the way to Wickcliffe I passed several historical markers to events of the Civil War and one to the French explorer, Robert De La Salle. He and others were canoeing down the Mississippi in 1682 seeking the mouth of the river; being commissioned by Louis the Fourteenth of France. The Ohio river that joins the Mississippi close by was proclaimed by La Salle on April 9th 1682 to be the northern watershed of the new province of Louisiana, of the French colonial empire.

The most intriguing historical item was a mile later, the Wickliffe Mounds. There are several mounds in the area peopled from about 800 AD and known as the Mississippian Culture. These Indians were active farmers on the rich soil close to the river. From about 1500 AD they left for reasons still not understood. The Wickliffe Mounds were first mapped in 1880 and excavated from the 1930's onwards. The museum had an extensive array of artefacts from the excavations, but for me the most interesting sight was the excavated mounds exposing the burial chambers of the dead.

A little further and I walked over the Ohio river bridge into Cairo. Two motels refused to let me stay—the first and only time this happened—and the third gave me a room. Again I had walked too far but felt very pleased with my performance. I was sorry to leave Kentucky, for I had come to love it!

OHIO BRIDGE—MISSISSIPPI BRIDGE IN BACKGROUND

MISSOURI

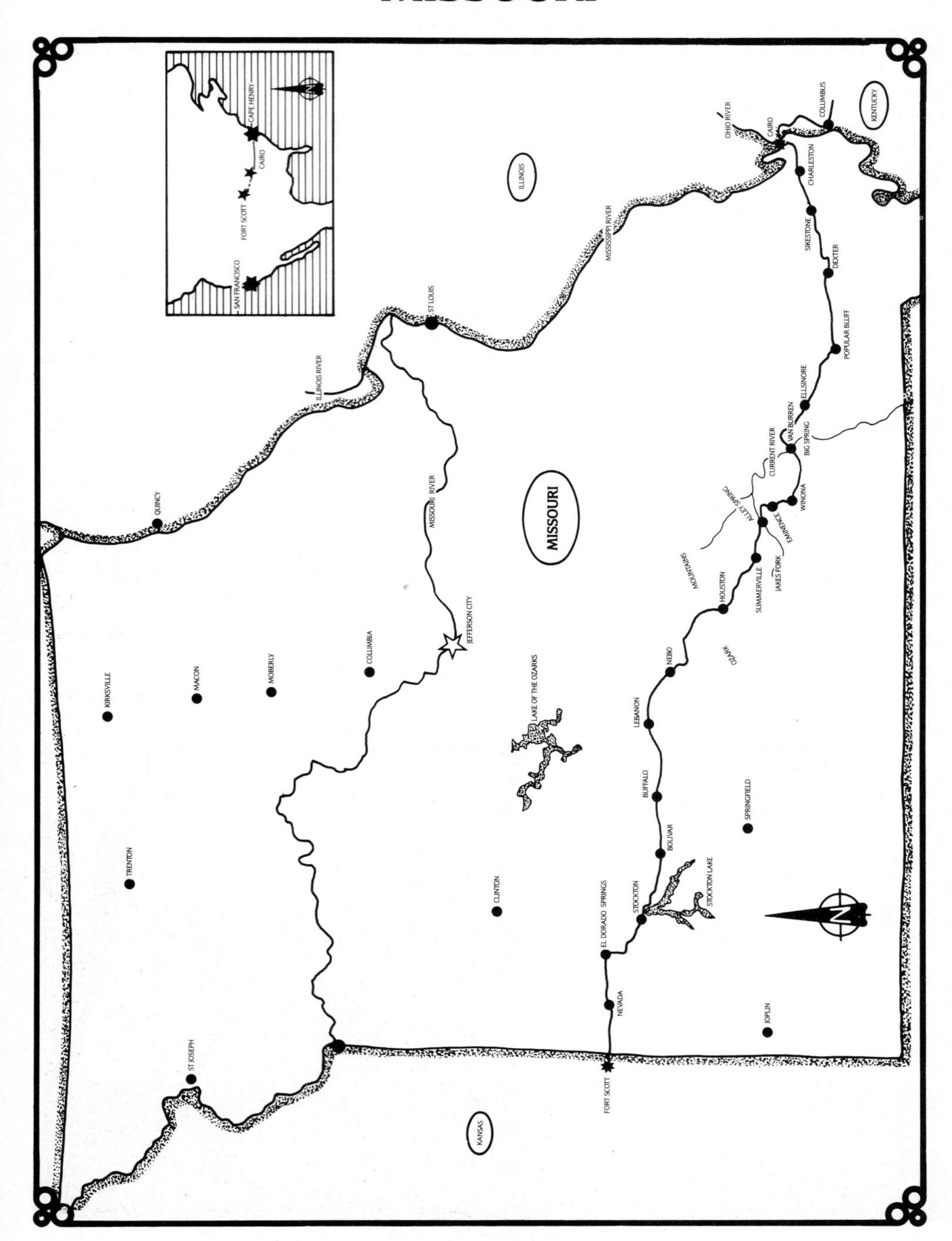
CAPE HENRY
CAIRO
FORT SCOTT
SAN FRANCISCO
ILLINOIS
KENTUCKY
OHIO RIVER
CAIRO
COLUMBUS
CHARLESTON
SIKESTONE
DEXTER
POPULAR BLUFF
ELLSINORE
VAN BURREN
BIG SPRING
CURRENT RIVER
WINONA
ALLEY SPRING
EMINENCE
MOUNTAINS
SUMMERVILLE
JAKES FORK
HOUSTON
OZARK
NEBO
LEBANON
BUFFALO
BOLIVAR
SPRINGFIELD
STOCKTON LAKE
STOCKTON
EL DORADO SPRINGS
NEVADA
JOPLIN
FORT SCOTT
KANSAS
ST JOSEPH
TRENTON
CLINTON
KIRKSVILLE
MACON
MOBERLY
COLUMBIA
JEFFERSON CITY
LAKE OF THE OZARKS
MISSOURI
MISSOURI RIVER
QUINCY
ILLINOIS RIVER
ST LOUIS
MISSISSIPPI RIVER
N

MISSOURI—THE 'SHOW ME STATE'.

State motto—'Let the good (or welfare) of the people be the supreme law.'

CAPITAL—JEFFERSON CITY

POPULATION—(1980 CENSUS) 4,917,444

HIGHEST ELEVATION—TAUM SAUK MOUNTAIN, 1,772 FEET.

LOWEST ELEVATION—EXTREME SOUTH END OF THE LOWLANDS, 230 FEET.

TOTAL AREA—19TH IN SIZE—69,674 SQUARE MILES

STATE BIRD—BLUEBIRD

STATE TREE—FLOWERING DOGWOOD

STATE FLOWER—HAWTHORN

The 24th state admitted to the Union in 1821. In 1803 Napolean Bonaparte had sold the Louisiana Territory to the United States for $15,000,000. The state is a major producer of vehicles and aircraft and three quaters of land is devoted to some kind of farming; this includes about 12,000,000 acres of forest. There are 19,050 miles of rivers and streams and 1,100 natural springs.

JOHN MERRILL AND MISSOURI STATE SIGN

DAY 43—
CAIRO (ILLINOIS) TO MINER (MISSOURI)—
33 MILES (1,058 MILES)

Cairo was once an important port at the junction of the Ohio and Mississippi rivers. The large warehouses and grain stores were once thriving with people but today it is largely a thing of the past. There were many people out of work and the whole place looked as though it had seen better days. I left early, shortly after 6.0a.m., and walked out of the city to cross the Mississippi bridge. Like the Ohio bridge it was more than a mile long and narrow; just enough room for two vehicles and no pedestrian! I took my life in my hands as I crossed, flattening myself against the barrier when a truck passed by. Fortunately they were working on the bridge and vehicle traffic was restricted to a single lane. I caused a stir as I insisted on walking across and the traffic operator spoke on his two way radio and stopped the traffic while I walked across! It took me over twenty minutes. I imagined irate Americans having to wait for a pedestrian and hid once I reached the other side!

At the Missouri state sign I did my usual ritual of putting the camera on the rucksack and running backwards and forwards and smiling. Close by were numerous firework stalls. July 4th, Independance Day, was a few days ahead. I saw none in Kentucky as state law forbids the sale of fireworks. Everyone who wants some has to drive over the state line to Missouri; they appeared to be doing a roaring trade.

Missouri was an instant contrast to Kentucky, being very flat with considerable farmlands. Soya beans were growing—America exports $9 billion worth to Japan. The road curved its way far into the distance and I had to forget it, except that the roads had no shoulder and the drivers didn't like a hiker, pounding their horns vigorously as they approached; often I had to jump out of the way. I followed Highway 60/62 to Wyatt and Charleston to Miner where I stopped. I chastised myself for walking too much; back into the 90's again.

SOYA BEAN FIELD

DAY 44— MINER TO DEXTER— 33 MILES(1,091 MILES)

At Sikeston just beyond Miner, I left Highway 60 and followed the smaller Highway 114. I couldn't stand 60 anymore from the inconsiderate drivers. Although this was a longer way to Dexter it was more peaceful and into the farmland of Stoddard county. Soya beans were again prominent but there were some massive rice fields with major irrigation schemes. Later I passed extensive corn plantations with young plants which were now over three feet tall. The rice fields amazed me with their size. To see a field over fifty acres in size after having walked in the Himalayas and seen the three foot wide terraces, was almost beyond comprehension.

After twenty miles I stopped at a small diner in Essex. Everyone inside was a farmer with checked shirt, jeans and cowboy boots. How one walked across, a ploughed field in those I just can't imagine. It was obviously lunch break, for they tucked heartily into hamburgers and drank beer straight from the bottle. I had a hamburger and coke. Outside the temperature was 94 degrees and I seemed at last to be getting used to the heat for I appeared to walk well and not get listless as the day wore on. I hate wearing anything on my head but I did carry a small cap and occasionally I wore it but only when my forehead became too sore. I carried sun cream but hardly ever remembered to put it on.

Approaching Dexter was a surprise as it was situated on a small ridge overlooking the surrounding area. Nearing the City park a jeep pulled up and out jumped a fit looking male. We shook hands and he explained he had done a bit of hiking on the Appalachian Trail. I explained my route and after five minutes he drove on. Three minutes later he was back; 'would I like somewhere to stay and wash?' Yes I would and he explained his parents' house was four miles away, thankfully on my route. He left to tell his mother, and I walked on.

Two hours later in almost desperation having ended up walking in the opposite direction, he found me, apologising for sending me the wrong way! James took me back to the house, which was just like he described, 'like the Alamo.' Being small windowed and almost Spanish in style. Here was an American family with everything. A large house, paddock with horses, a car or jeep each, a couple of planes, a satellite dish, a 45" colour television set, and the incessant phone. I showered and changed into some of James' shorts while mine were washed. We climbed aboard his jeep and toured the area. First to see his father's concrete plant and examples of their work, before visiting the airport and seeing the planes. Next, rather to cause a stir among his friends we 'cruised main street' eyeing the girls! Usually one goes to the next town to do this, and the males from that town come to yours to cruise. We returned to 'the Alamo' and met the whole of the Sites family before eating dinner. By 10p.m. I fell asleep from the hard walk and the excitement of the day.

RICE FIELDS

DAY 45—DEXTER TO POPULAR BLUFF—29 MILES (1,120 MILES)

The Sites family were all up early, and after a French toast breakfast I was the last person to leave, just after 6.30a.m.! On their advice I cut across the golf course to join Highway 60 again. For a while the traffic thundered past, but at Fisk I followed the old and quieter road to Popular Bluff. Although a flat landscape there was plenty to see, with more huge expanses of corn, soya beans and rice growing. Around noon the air was shattered by the swooping and droning of a crop—spraying plane.Whilst the pilot was performing an important task, I could not help but appreciate how much the pilot was enjoying himself. He flew just above the crops before pulling the joy stick back to climb up steeply before circling and coming in low again. A flag bearing truck moved each pass so the pilot knew which section to spray next.

I reached downtown area of Popular Bluff feeling quite tired. I was a bit annoyed at myself for doing another 30 mile day. It must stop, for in the end you burn yourself up. But I was pleased at my performance, despite 94 degrees again, and the boots had now totally surrendered to my feet and were causing no pain or blisters. My body was complaining at averaging 30 miles a day for the last week and, although I resolved to ease off, the logical stopping points on the walk meant for the next few days I walked around 23 miles a day.

93 DEGREES, POPULAR BLUFF

DAY 46—
POPULAR BLUFF TO ELLSINORE—
24 MILES (1,144 MILES)

I was off shortly after dawn, first along the dual-laned Highway 60/67, heading north before turning left onto Highway 60 and heading west. Here I entered the Mark Twain National Forest. All the time I was walking I kept pondering on how to get some money.Today was Friday and I had $28 left. The nearest American Express office was at Springfield, Missouri, about 180 miles away. At first I thought I could walk there and make the money last, but I needed a minimum of $10 a day to keep myself on the road. I decided that I would have to hitch a lift to Springfield and return the next day. I hated the thought of doing this but felt I had no option.

By lunchtime I reached Ellsinore and put my thumb out. Within ten minutes a car stopped and took me to Mountain View. I had to wait five minutes before another car stopped. This turned out to be Terry, who had been leading a canoe party on the Current River.He proved an admirable companion and understood what I was doing. He drove hard along the major highway and I was glad not to be walking it. I resolved to take another route from Ellsinore across Missouri to the north of Springfield. Fortunately, Terry knew Springfield well and took me straight to the downtown mall where the American Express office was. We had half an hour to spare and I cashed a cheque for $750. The controller informed that I should have been able to withdraw money at the bank I called at in Kentucky.

Obviously, I couldn't get back to Ellsinore that night, and Terry very kindly offered a settee to sleep at his house, which he shared with three others in Springfield. That night we went out and ate our way through a huge home cooked pizza, while I listened to Terry telling me about the Ozarks, its trail, natural springs and river. I couldn't wait to get there.

BIG SPRING

DAY 47—ELLSINORE TO VAN BURREN—22 MILES (1,166 MILES)

Terry returned me to Highway 60 where we parted firm friends. Within five minutes I had got a lift in a magnificent 4 × 4 driven by a trucker who had his own business in Springfield. He took me to Willow Springs. On the way we saw a couple of Amrths who have a similar life to the Shakers and Quakers. It was like seeing America a century ago as they rode beside the highway in a pony and trap, with the women in long dresses and bonnet hats, and the men in tweed suits and beards. They were very well respected in the area and renowned for their hard work on their land. Their homes have no electricity or television.

The first car I hitched in Willow Springs stopped and the elderly driver took me all the way back to Ellsinore, which I reached at just after 11a.m. I was glad to back on my route again although slightly off-put by seeing a bit of the road I would now be walking along. I was soon back in my stride and glad to be walking again with money in my pocket. By teatime I entered Van Burren and got the last room in the motel. Being a Saturday and a lovely sunny day the place was full of people. The motel owners were most interested in my walk and gave me a lift down to see the famous Big Spring.

In Missouri there are more than 1,100 known natural springs, and Big Spring is the biggest with an average of 227 million gallons a day bursting out of the surface. It has been known to go as high as 846 million gallons. The area is particularly scenic with the crystal clear water and forest and is part of the Ozark National Scenic Riverway, which includes the Current and Jacks Fork rivers. Canoe trips are a very pleasant way of exploring the area but by far the favourite short trip was a float down the river on a rubber tube or raft. Cooling in the water or in an ice chest would be beer and coke. I was envious, and I would see more of the riverway system and the Ozarks over the next few days.

I waited for the motel truck to appear to pick up another batch of floaters and jumped on board for the ride back to Van Burren. Back in the motel I began to shower when I heard a banging noise. I hadn't realised how thin the walls were. At first I thought someone was knocking a nail in but when the knocking increased its tempo and moans began to rip the air I knew exactly what was going on! How off putting, I had been away from my wife for seven weeks and was now living a celibate lifestyle!

FLOATING RIVER, NR VAN BURREN

DAY 48—VAN BURREN TO WINONA—22 MILES (1,188 MILES)

I left at 6.0.a.m. and was surprised at how cool it was; no doubt because of the river. The night before I tracked down a copy of the Ozark Trail booklet and debated whether to use it. A 500 mile Ozark Trail is planned and a thirty mile section near Van Burren is detailed in the booklet. After a lot of searching I found the trail and saw it was little used and hard to follow. I was in two minds anyway—it would take me away from my projected line and entail an extra 30 miles. I pressed on on Highway 60 past fields full of large bales of hay and others covered in a blaze of buttercups. A mile or so later I passed Sassafrass City. At first I walked on, but seeing an unusual sign I backtracked and photographed the population figures.

I was now back into another section of the Mark Twain National Forest with elegant pines offering shade from the sun. As the day wore on I felt tired, and after eight hours having nothing to eat or drink I entered Winona and turned right onto Highway 19. Seeing a motel I decided to call it a day. I had walked 192 miles in the last 7 days, which was far more than planned. At first I could find no one at the motel but eventually awoke the owner. He was suffering from a hangover after being taken out by a lady friend! He obligingly cooked a meal for me as his restaurant was closed being Sunday. I tucked into a huge plate of French fries and a couple of hamburgers. Afterwards I sat in the sun and oiled my boots—something I rarely do but the continuous dry weather had made the leather particularly dry. I quickly dropped a line to Sheila, noting this was the first of July.

SASSAFRASS CITY BOARD

DAY 49—WINONA TO ALLEY SPRING—22 MILES (1,210 MILES)

Wanted to be off early but the restaurant didn't open until 7 a.m. Anyway it was good to have a couple of eggs and hash browns again. The highway was quiet and passed through attractive scenery, and I was slowly falling in love with the Ozarks and its springs, rivers, woodlands and rolling hills. Eminence turned out to be an attractive town and at the post office there I sent a pile of maps and papers back to Britain. I now headed westwards on Highway 106 towards Alley Spring. The hills were quite steep and at the top of the biggest one was a wayside rest-stop with a food stall. The owner watched me walk in dripping with sweat from the climb and immediately gave me a massive glass of ice cold lemon to drink. Refreshed, she said that would be $1.50!

I declined another and pressed on to Alley Spring. Here was a beautiful campsite near Jacks Fork river and I couldn't resist stopping although it was only early afternoon. It was good to set the tent up, and, with thoughts of a salad tea I skipped along the road to visit Alley Spring. This spring is the fourth biggest in the State and averages 81 million gallons a day (307 million litres). The spring pool is a rich green colour and the water is still used to drive the adjacent Red Mill for grinding corn. It was always embarrassing to be asked where I was walking to and from. Entering the building with my boots and bronzed physique I was immediately asked what I was doing. 'Walking to the Pacific', I glibly replied, 'about 1,200 miles so far'. She was speechless at first but said ' as you have walked so far to here you had better see the mill working.' Whereupon the sluice gates were opened and wheels began to turn and some corn was ground.

Walking back to the tent I saw numerous people floating on the river and held back from doing the same. I had still not fully relaxed and adjusted to the task. At the shop I purchased the ingredients for a sardine salad and several cans of beer. Seeing a Missouri badge I decided to buy it and I bought one for every state that I walked through—not to sew on my rucksack but to frame upon my return. After a long hot shower I lay outside the tent and demolished the salad and beer. By 7 p.m. I was fast asleep.

ALLEY MILL

DAY 50—ALLEY SPRING TO YUKON—28 MILES (1,238 MILES)

Just after 6 a.m. with the tent down I strapped my rucksack on once more and set off; no one else was awake yet. I continued through forest on Highway 106 to Summerville, passing Flat Rock look out tower. I couldn't resist the temptation of ascending the numerous steps to get a view over the Ozarks. Missouri had come as a surprise and I hadn't expected to see such good scenery here. The view was simply over ridge and hill covered with trees.

I pressed on to Summerville where I entered Texas county and followed Highway 17 to Yukon. The last few days the temperature had been in the low 80's but today it rocketed to 95 degrees. The heat was not bothering me as I passed out of forest into farmland following straight roads. In Yukon there was no motel or anywhere to camp and a local shop owner drove me to Houston; the capital of Texas county! How unoriginal can you get. There I stayed in a motel and was visited by a reporter from the Summersville paper.I had only just arrived in time, for a violent thunderstorm moved in but an hour later the sun was shining on the glistening streets. That night I rang Sheila for the first time for days.

OZARK LAKE

DAY 51—YUKON TO LICKING—19 MILES (1,257 MILES)

I soon got a lift back to Yukon and followed Highway 137 to Licking. The weather had certainly changed from being dry and sunny to being cold and raining. Last night's storm had returned and for much of the day it thundered and flashed, while water streamed down. It was July 4th and I had hoped to attend some Independence Day celebrations but the weather had cancelled them. Instead, upon reaching Licking I stayed in a motel and watched other places in America in the sun enjoying and celebrating their National holiday. In fact in the evening it rained so hard and so long that I didn't even venture out for a meal.

TEXAS COUNTY

DAY 52—LICKING TO NEBO—
36 MILES (1,293 MILES)

I was eager to be off after having an easy day forced onto me yesterday and was walking before 6.0a.m.The weather too was back to normal—dry and sunny—and reached 92 degrees in the afternoon. I never intended to walk so much this day but circumstances dictated otherwise. First it was along Highway 30 towards Success but seeing I would be walking far out of my way I decided to cut through the forest on minor roads to Roby. The walking was excellent, being in remote country and away from major roads and cars. First I headed into Pine Creek Wilderness and crossed Pine Creek. Beautiful forest with a rock escarpment above the wide creek. A couple were canoeing down it, obviously camping on the way from the amount of gear that was stored aboard. We couldn't converse but simply waved to each other.

On the map was marked a Merrill cemetery. I searched in vain, and pressed on up the track to Sandwood and the Big Piney Trail which I followed for a short while before gaining Roby in early afternoon. I sat outside the store and drank ½ gallon of milk. Here I rejoined Highway 32, which was a very minor road, and continued westwards to Plato where a local informed me there was a campsite at Lynchburg 4 miles away and on my route. I reached there late afternoon and saw no campsite. The store was about to close and the owners were not very helpful and confirmed there was no campsite here. Opposite was a particularly attractive expanse of lawn but they refused to give me permission to camp. I had now walked 30 miles but felt I would have to press on and hopefully find somewhere to camp.

As I walked I looked at barns and places to camp but was reluctant to ask a farmer for permission to camp. For me this was a sign I was over tired but I continued walking. After another hour I reached a church and debated whether to camp there but couldn't bring myself to stop. I began to feel desperate and an hour later at a little after 8 p.m., after 14 hours of continuous walking, I saw a family sitting outside their house. I enquired if there was anywhere to camp, and they replied as if answering a prayer, on the lawn here! The Hannray family made me most welcome and quickly cooked me a meal which I ate slowly before falling asleep.

PINE CREEK

DAY 53—NEBO TO LEBANON— 26 MILES (1,319 MILES)

The Hannray family were all up before 6 a.m. and two of the sons had already left for work; one on a farm and the other to a truck driving school. I joined the parents for breakfast and they very kindly made me a cheese sandwich to eat later in the day. I was sorry to leave such hospitable people.It never ceases to amaze me that wherever I walk 'something' always materialises at the right moment. The route to Lebanon was all along Highway 32, first through the western edge of Mark Twain's National Forest and over the Gasconade River before the Osage Fork river.

I was not walking well, the effort of yesterday had left me drained and listless. I broke my rules and kept stopping at gas stations and stores for a drink and a rest. Nearing Lebanon the road become a major highway and entering the city a storm and heavy rain descended. Finding a motel I fell exhausted onto the bed. That night I weighed myself and found I had lost 21 pounds and now weighed 152 pounds. The walk was surely a crazy way to lose weight. Whilst jeans and T shirts were the normal attire for the men there was an increasing number wearing cowboy boots and hats.

COWBOY

DAY 54—LEBANON TO BUFFALO—30 MILES (1,349 MILES)

In the motel reception it was frustrating to see the brochures about the Lake of the Ozarks to the north of here. Sadly there was never enough time to explore off my route but the day's walk passed through very pleasant countryside, a mixture of hills, woodlands and farmland. I kept on Highway 32 all day, and on setting out the sky looked dull and forbidding. Half an hour later it thundered and lightning flashed for a few minutes while I sheltered in a barn. I continued, hoping it had blown away, but infact it was just a momentary pause before the storm came back with greater intensity. Fortunately I had reached a church and sat in the porch while it streamed with rain for over two hours. I had bought a large packet of candy drops, so I ate the lot!

Once it had stopped raining I continued, although thunder still rolled around. An hour later the sun appeared and by the end of the day it had topped 88 degrees. At Long Lane—the only place on the route, although it had definitely seen more prosperous times—the bank had the date 1920 on and looked like a western set, while the wooden building opposite was abandoned and a dummy swung from an upper window with a noose around its neck.I reached Buffalo close to the major Highway 65, feeling very tired, after walking 12 hours. There were three motels, the first two were full and in the last one I secured the last room. I knew I was pushing it too much and, as I noted in my diary, I must slow down!

LONG LANE

DAY 55—BUFFALO TO BOLIVAR—20 MILES—(1,369 MILES)

In an effort to take things easier I tried to set off later and watch a bit of breakfast television, such as Good Morning America, but I simply felt too restless and left! I continued on Highway 32, first to Half Way, although this was certainly not my half way point of the day. Before reaching there a dog must have felt he wanted to go for a walk for he simply followed me on the other side of the road for four miles. In the end he just dropped to the ground and lay there panting as I walked on.

I thought Bolivar would be a good place to stop, being the capital of Polk county with a population of 6,000 people. I arrived mid afternoon and was surprised not to find a motel. In the end I began walking out on Highway 32—the right way of my route but the wrong way for motels! I had only been walking twenty minutes when a sports car drew up. The driver was drinking a can of beer but seemed friendly and offered to drive me to a motel. I accepted and in a couple of minutes was at a motel with pool. My driver suggested I could come round for a meal that evening and would ring. True to his word, half an hour later he rang and said he would pick me up at six. So began an enjoyable aquaintance with the Beaman family.

At six a car pulled up, Mr Beaman thought I might appreciate a ride in a British car—a 1957 MGA. When I informed him I had a couple of MGB's and had at one time owned an MGA Twin Cam, we became instant friends. The car was in immaculate condition and was his pride and joy. His home was a magnificent wooden colonial styled building full of character. I met his wife Janice who turned out to be a reporter for the Bolivar Free Press and later she interviewed me for the paper. We were joined by a couple of neigbours and pulled the tabs off a few cans of Coors beer before sitting down to an 18 oz steak. The best Sunday evening meal I had had for some time. In the cool of the evening I was driven back to the motel in the open topped sports car.

HALF-WAY

DAY 56—BOLIVAR TO STOCKTON—
28 MILES (1,397 MILES)

In the morning I retraced my steps back into downtown Bolivar and called at the Gold Rush for breakfast. Who should be dining there but Mrs Beaman! She was off to the paper to write my story and hoped to catch me up later to take a few photographs of me 'on location'. She arrived an hour later when I was on my way to Fair Play on Highway 32.

The temperature was now becoming increasingly hotter each day although I did not appreciate at the time how close I was to Kansas. The day peaked at 96 degrees with high humidity. I was still in vacation country with Pomme De Terre Lake to the north and Stockton Lake just to the south. I was now really settling into the walk and walking well, and my feet never complained and were now covered by hard skin. From experience I found you have to walk about 1,500 miles on a major walk before you really have adjusted to your task and are at one with the countryside. In Stockton I stayed at Halliday Motel at a cost of $14, which included a Queen sized bed, colour TV, bath (tub) and outdoor pool. The latter I could not resist after such a hot day, and I lay in it for half an hour before watching the Miss Universe Pageant on television. The winner was Miss Sweden who was my second choice.

STOCKSTILL GROCERY

DAY 57—
STOCKTON TO EL DORADO SPRINGS—
23 MILES (1,420 MILES)

I set off in high spirits for I knew Kansas was only a couple of days away and at El Dorado Springs there should be mail for me. The heat soon reached 95 degrees and I hoped at Filley on Highway 32 to get something to eat. All the shops were selling antiques and I had to make do with a couple of cokes from a machine. I walked hard with the thoughts of mail and reached the Post Office early afternoon. There were three letters from Sheila. I headed back to Highway 54 and checked into the C & H Motel who were full of interest in my stroll.

I felt in a reckless mood and purchased a quart of milk from the store next door, then put my feet up on a sun-lounger and read my mail. I took a swig of milk and spat it out; it was off! The store were full of apologies and gave me another. Back on the lounger I enjoyed the cold drink while I read letters from Sheila which made me emotional. I hurried out for a meal and watched television to take my mind off-things.

EL DORADO SPRINGS POST OFFICE

BUSHWHACKER MUSEUM

DAY 58—
EL DORADO SPRINGS TO NEVADA—
22 MILES (1,442 MILES)

At first I thought we were in for another thunderous day as menacing clouds hung over the area. I needn't have worried—the clouds soon evaporated and the temperature topped 90, again. My route was due west along Highway 54 to Nevada. The day was to prove a most interesting one, not only my final day in Missouri, but a curtain raiser for Kansas.

After eight miles I stopped at a gas station in Dederick for a pint of milk. I drank it inside and noticed in the window a hog carrier. Apparently the owner made them himself and was doing a roaring trade. The design was simple; a wooden frame with carrying handle. The instructions were to the point—1. Place head of hog through hole provided. 2. Screw winged screw into hole provided under tail!

Entering Nevada I saw you could camp in the park but was worried about leaving my gear for much of the afternoon, while I explored the city, so I checked into a motel. Removing my T shirt for a wash I was horrified to see myself in the mirror. The upper part of my body was covered in bites. Apparently I had been bitten by the 'Missouri bug'.

I headed into Main Street to look for the Bushwhacker Museum armed with a piece of paper about it, saying—

> 'For some ninety years this stone building meant 'durance vile' to assorted 'Border Ruffians'—those colorful, cutthroat characters who kept lawmen busy for a whole generation along Missouri's brawling, turbulent western frontier. See the old cell room where their scrawled signatures, drawings and escape attempts can still be traced, and you, too, will know what 'durance vile' means!'

Seeing the building I knew I had at last entered the real west and I certainly would not have liked to have been a prisoner in those small cells; I soon appreciated that it was considered the 'worst jail in the State.' It was in use from 1855 until December 1960. The term Bushwhacker refers to a Confederate guerrilla and in the Civil War Nevada was known as the 'Bushwhacker Capital.'

There were many items to look at but unfortunately the custodians were more interested in what I was doing. A chair was quickly pulled out so that I could rest, 'after walking so far!' The press were rung and within five minutes a reporter from the Nevada Daily Mail appeared. He also did a recording for KNEM radio. The reporter was proud of his area and insisted on showing me around. We toured the streets and visited Radio Springs Park whose natural springs were well known to the Osage Indians. We cruised around the cemetery, mostly in a car, looking at gravestones trying to find some to the early settlers. The highlight for me was visiting a farm nearby where an agricultural conference was taking place in a field of soya beans. Again I was the centre of attraction. That evening the reporter and his wife took me out for a meal—steak ofcourse. A more fitting end to my walk across Missouri would be hard to find. Kansas tomorrow; I slept solidly.

KANSAS

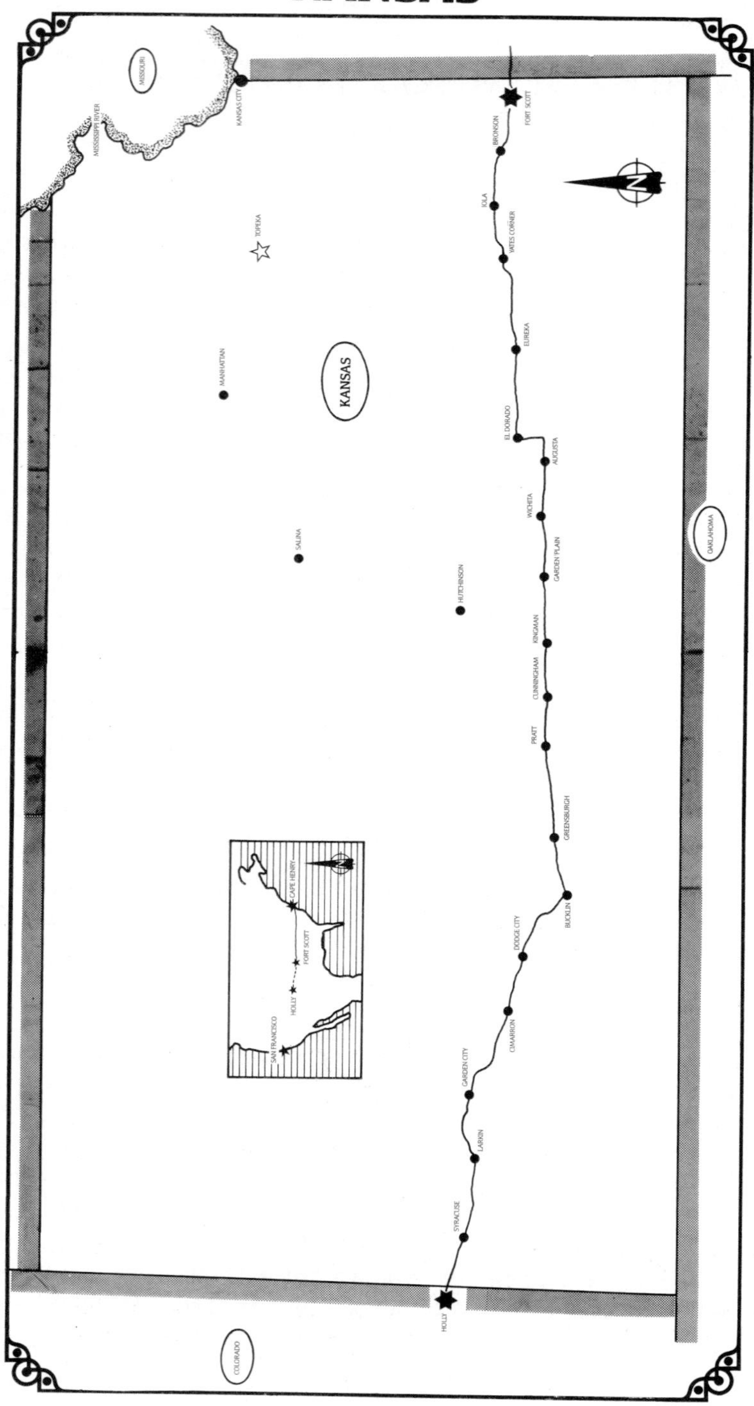

MISSOURI
MISSISSIPPI RIVER
KANSAS CITY
TOPEKA
MANHATTAN
KANSAS
SALINA
HUTCHINSON
FORT SCOTT
BRONSON
IOLA
YATES CORNER
EUREKA
EL DORADO
AUGUSTA
WICHITA
GARDEN PLAIN
KINGMAN
CUNNINGHAM
PRATT
GREENSBURGH
BUCKLIN
DODGE CITY
CIMARRON
GARDEN CITY
LARKIN
SYRACUSE
HOLLY
COLORADO
OAKLAHOMA
CAPE HENRY
FORT SCOTT
HOLLY
SAN FRANCISCO

KANSAS—THE SUNFLOWER STATE—

State motto—'To the stars through difficulties.'

CAPITAL—TOPEKA

POPULATION—(1970 CENSUS)—2,249,071

HIGHEST ELEVATION—4,026 FEET

LOWEST ELEVATION—700 FEET

TOTAL AREA—82,264 SQUARE MILES

STATE BIRD—WESTERN MEADOW LARK

STATE TREE—COTTONWOOD—often called 'the pioneer tree of Kansas'.

STATE FLOWER—SUNFLOWER

STATE SONG—HOME ON THE RANGE

AVERAGE ANNUAL RAINFALL—26.43 INCHES

Kansas is often referred to as the 'Breadbasket of the Nation', with its huge expanses of wheat and massive cattle stations. Historically it is the start of the west with famous trails such as the Santa Fe Trail, Oregon Trail and Chisholm Trails. It is also the midway state of America. Famous Kansans include Buffalo Bill, Wyatt Earp, Wild Bill Hickock and Dwight D. Eisenhower.

JOHN MERRILL AND KANSAS STATE SIGN

DAY 59—NEVADA (MISSOURI) TO FORT SCOTT (KANSAS)—23 MILES (1,465 MILES)

I left early, eager to get to Kansas. At first the road was dual-laned but after five miles became single. I had now left the hills and forest behind, entering very flat country. Everyone I had talked to about walking across Kansas had been alarmed. All said it would be hot and all I would see would be waving wheat. It was simply a question of speed! In fact it was hot but a most interesting state full of history, but no waving wheat, as the combines had been through three weeks before! As for sunflowers I saw many but not as many as I was to see in Colorado.

At the Stateline I called at a store and celebrated by drinking a couple of cans of Dr. Pepper. Donning my cap to shade my nose once more from the rays of the sun I posed beside the Kansas sign while the camera clicked away on the time exposure, secured to the fence. Jubilant I headed on to Fort Scott. Whilst the feeling of full adjustment to the walk had been bubbling up for the last few days, entering Kansas released my euphoria and I knew at last I was well on my way and very optomistic about the outcome.

I checked into a motel before buying a couple of films to photograph Fort Scott. Even the best laid plans get waylaid as word soon spread of an English coast to coast hiker. A reporter from the Fort Scott Tribune appeared and I told my story before visiting the fort. The fort dates back to 1842 and cost $32,000 to construct. It served as a base for the U.S. Army's peace-keeping efforts on the 'permanent Indian frontier.' The fort had links with other well known forts such as Leavenworth, Laramie and Bent's Fort which I was to reach on the other side of Kansas. The whole complex of 18 buildings have been beautifully restored and cared for by the National Park Service.

Dragoons from the fort fought in two major battles of the Mexican War in the 1840's. The next decade saw many atrocities associated with slavery which became known as 'Bleeding Kansas.' And in the 1860's was involved in the Civil War. In 1863 there were 350 wagons, 400 horses, 2200 mules and 460 men here. I took a whole film of the various buildings before resting in the shade.

FORT SCOTT

DAY 60—FORT SCOTT TO BRONSON—22 MILES (1,487 MILES)

I should have known that things would go wrong today but it wasn't until late afternoon that I realised it was Friday the 13th. Being superstitious I should have taken more care. However I set off on Highway 54. The road was straight and could be seen for long stretches ahead but this did not put me off. After ten miles I was sweating profusely and I stopped at a gas station for a drink. The temperature was into the 90's already.

I pressed on feeling listless and hot, leaving a trail of sweat drops along the road side. I entered Bronson just after 2 p.m. and was surprised to find no motel. I went into a store to cool down and drank half a gallon of milk and a couple of sodas. There was nowhere to camp and no one would give me permission to do so. I stayed in the store for an hour slowly regaining normality. A woman opposite was sympathetic and said I was probably suffering from the heat. I didn't think so—it was only 92 degrees, so I thought. In fact it was 104—no wonder I was feeling off colour!

The woman, Marjorie Schultz, said she was getting a taxi to the next town, Iola, and I was very welcome to have a lift to a motel. I hadn't the heart to refuse. An hour later I was lying in a pool feeling decidedly much better! The heat had worried me but as the walk progressed it was the one and only time that it affected me. I hadn't also realised that the humidity was so high—at least 80%, which also took its toll on me. I resolved that perhaps I had better start carrying some fluid, and, if the heat got worse, I had better walk at night. As I wrote in my log that night, 'So begins the tough crux of the walk to the cool Rockies.'

DOWNTOWN, FORT SCOTT

DAY 61—BRONSON TO IOLA—
18 MILES (1,505 MILES)

I soon got a lift back to Bronson and walked to Iola 18 miles away, where I had stayed. Again it was hot, and by afternoon it reached 106 but I had no side effects from it. I decided also that I had better adopt new tactics for Kansas by being off at dawn and getting to my destination by 2 p.m. before the temperature peaked. However, I literally ran along the road for I had at last reached my magical figure of 1,500 miles. To celebrate I had my boots reheeled at a cost of only $5. With road walking so much I was finding the vibram heel only lasted 750 miles.

I went slightly mad also and purchased a new pair of shorts, for 'best', as the ones I was wearing were now very faded, although they did last five months of wear! I even purchased a quart bottle to carry liquid in. And I astounded myself by washing all my clothes! That night I went to a Pizza Hut to celebrate in my new white shorts.

Earlier in the afternoon I explored Iola which has a huge central square, the largest in the U.S. I was proudly told. Just off Main Street was the Allen County jail and museum. Like the one in Nevada, it was complete with cells and very uncomfortable beds. The building dates from 1869 and was in use for 90 years.

ALLEN COUNTY JAIL

DAY 62—BRONSON TO YATES CENTRE—22 MILES (1,527 MILES)

I was up before dawn at 5.0a.m. adopting my new Kansan routine. Following breakfast at McDonalds I hit the road—Highway 54—a really straight road, and after ten miles I could see Yates Centre 12 miles away! Typically, when one prepares for something the problem resolves itself and one's effort is not needed. Instead of the anticipated searing 100 degrees heat, it was actually cool, cloudy and lightly raining! Walking was a real pleasure passing fields, hedges and a few trees and a pond ablaze with white lilies. There was no gas station or store on the way.

I entered Yates Centre in drizzle just before 2.0p.m., the town's sign proudly displaying—The Hay capital of the World. The surrounding area is also known for its quail and prairie chicken hunting. As with my new theme there was a museum, a log cabin and a historic square to explore. In an ice-cream stall I disgraced myself by demolishing the biggest banana split I and the others had ever seen. While waiting to be served a man kept staring at my legs. Eventually he commented that he had never seen such large calf muscles before. I must admit they were bulging, and being deeply tanned I looked in peak physical condition. He asked how I got them, simply by walking, I replied; not letting on how far I had walked!

WATER LILIES

DAY 63—YATES CENTRE TO EUREKA—32 MILES (1,559 MILES)

I looked forward to the next couple of days with mixed feelings for I knew both would be over thirty miles and, if the heat topped 100 degrees, it would be hard. However, as I crossed the Flint Hills, the last true prairie of America, the weather was in my favour. The wheat had all been cut and, although now mid July, it was cool and only 89 degrees. I left shortly after 6a.m., following very straight roads, Highway 54, over the gentle hills full of cattle, for this was cattle-fattening country. After 14 miles I passed near Toronto Lake, which has good fishing and was named by Canadian settlers.

At Neal, a small hamlet close to the road, I stopped and chatted to a man sitting outside his mechanical store. He didn't seem to have much business but he said his Bank was happy! He informed me that Highway 54 was the most direct road across Kansas and in this area used by 1,600 cars a day. As the cars passed I looked at the number plates to see where they had come from; only one was from California. I pressed on tired, but determined to reach Eureka 12 miles away. My face was badly burnt and I still could not bring myself to wear my cap or put sun cream on. I noticed that the hairs on my legs and arms had now turned blonde; if only the hair on my head would! The Eureka Downs are famous for horse racing and the annual purse is in excess of $200,000. I sought the refuge of a Motel for a long soak in a hot bath. That night I watched the start of the Democratic Convention, with Walter Mondale officially declaring Geraldine Ferraro as his running mate, to wild applause.

FLINT HILLS

DAY 64—EUREKA TO EL DORADO—30 MILES (1,589 MILES)

Again I was lucky, with the weather being cool and only into the mid—80's. Again I was following Highway 54 with the first 17 miles across the Flint Hills. At Rosalie after 20 miles I hoped for a store, but there was none and I had to wait until I gained a rest area shaded with cottonwood trees and drank ½ gallon of water.

My feet were now sore from the two day push and blisters were developing on my heels. I pressed on and, nearing the outskirts of El Dorado, saw a campground and camped. A nearby store gave me three home grown tomatoes, and together with a tin of tuna, I sat outside the tent and ate my salad, swilled down with a quart of orange juice and half a gallon of milk! By 6.30p.m. I was fast asleep.

HIGHWAY 54 AND GRAIN ELEVATOR

DAY 65—EL DORADO TO AUGUSTA—20 MILES (1,609 MILES)

Although refreshed from twelve hours sleep, I was still feeling the after effects of two days of hard walking. Three miles along the road brought me into downtown El Dorado, where I sat down to my biggest breakfast so far—2 eggs (over-easy), hash browns, 4 slices of toast, 3 mugs of coffee, and three hot cakes covered in maple syrup. Fortified, I headed south to Haverhill and Pickerell Corner, still following Highway 54 to Augusta.

Although I had now crossed the longest section, the heat returned and topped 96 degrees; glad it didn't yesterday. The last two days I had seen dozens of noddy pumps in the fields pumping crude oil 24hrs a day oil into tanks, which were regularly emptied. Ahead I could see the massive Getty oil refinery, recently sold for billions of dollars. I hadn't expected to see oil pumps in Kansas, just waving wheat, but the fields were cut. Another surprise of Kansas were the litter free roads. I would walk thirty miles of road and not see a discarded can. In other states I would see beer and coke cans galore and was always amazed to see McDonald's cups at least thirty miles away from their nearest restaurant.

I entered Augusta feeling very tired, and was glad to stop here and escape into an air conditioned room. My feet were still sore but the skin was very hard like an elephant's or a bare-foot porter's in Nepal. That night I kept up to date with the Democratic Convention. Mondale had won and Gary Hart and Jesse Jackson agreed to support the ticket.

OIL PUMP AND WELL

DAY 66—AUGUSTA TO WICHITA—22 MILES (1,631 MILES)

I was now approaching one of the biggest cities on my walk, Wichita. I was nervous, for I didn't want to get entangled with interstate roads, where you can't walk. In fact it was very easy to get into. First along the now dual-laned Highway 54. Although I wasn't short of money I knew there was an American Express office here and decided it would be prudent to stock up, after the 'Missouri dash'. I found Rock Road North and walked in. I don't think they had ever had a hiker before, never mind a coast to coast one! I was made most welcome, stocked up with dollars, and shown how to get into the downtown area.

My route was along Douglas Avenue past splendid houses, and, upon reaching the downtown area, celebrated by calling into McDonalds and having my 'dream snack'—big mac, coke, fries and strawberry shake. Although still tired, and it was 98 degrees outside, I decided to celebrate the fact that I was about half way across America but not half way on my route. Just down the road was the impressive circular Century 11 building and opposite a Holiday Inn. I couldn't resist it and went up the elevator. I checked in and no one commented on the extraordinary appearance of a hiker.

Wichita is the largest city in Kansas with a population of 276,554. Apart from major industries of meat packing, flour mills and oil refinery, it is the Air capital of the world, with major plants operated by Boeing,Cessna and Learjet. Close to the downtown area is Cow Town and I wished I had time to explore and the first buildings of Wichita and museums.

That night I put on clean shorts and T-shirt for eating out. Later I continued my TV update, first with the horror story of a gunman who went wild in a McDonalds in San Diego, killing 22 people. Next was Mondale's acceptance speech, which didn't impress me at all. Geraldine Ferraro gave an emotional one, and Senator Edward Kennedy showed his class and dominated the proceedings.

WICHITA, CENTURY 11 PLAZA

DAY 67—WICHITA TO GARDEN PLAIN—22 MILES (1,653 MILES)

I didn't wake up until 7.0a.m. and was immediately annoyed with myself for overlaying. Fifteen minutes later my rucksack was on my back once more as I pounded the tarmac! Three miles later I stopped at a McDonalds for breakfast. On the way I had passed the marker of the start of the Chisholm Trail—1865-1874. The trail was founded by Jesse Chisholm, and in the nine years it was in use more than 3,000,000 head of cattle arrived via this route. Later I passed Air Capital Memorial Park with a B11 bomber on a pedestal.

Getting into Wichita had been easy but the road out was unkind, being dual-laned and straight. The wheat fields were all cut, and in several places the stubble was being burnt. The air was certainly drier, which made walking more pleasant although it was 104 degrees. I followed Highway 54 to Goddard and Garden Plain, but there was nowhere to camp or stay there so I hitched a lift back to stay at a KOA campsite. As usual it lay 1½ miles off my route. I only wished there were more of these places on my route, for they certainly cater for the camper with store,washing facilities and a pool. I erected the tent in the shade before cooling off in the pool. Overall I was pleased with my performance, although I realised the heat was sapping my strength and I could not push myself as much as I can in the mountains. Of the two types of walking I felt cool mountain walking was by far the best.

B11 BOMBER

DAY 68—GARDEN PLAIN TO KINGMAN—22 MILES (1,675 MILES)

A camper returned me to Garden Plain and I pressed on along Highway 54, still dual-laned. Again it was hot, 103 degrees, but I was adjusting to it and carried no liquid. The cars that passed looked as though they were the early pioneer wagons, as the occupants had their air conditioning on full blast, the windows were tightly closed and towels fastened inside to deflect the sun. Walking was much easier. I could do nothing about it, whatever way you cross America heat in the middle is a problem, fortunately I had done no research so didn't appreciate this fact; had I done so I might have had second thoughts. It was now late July, and Kansas was enjoying its hottest weather and would not really cool down until September.

After twenty miles I neared Kingman and was relieved to see the dual-laned highway end and become a two-way road. In Kingman I was surprised to learn that San Francisco was now 1,721 miles away and Grand Canyon was 1,017. I was making progress after all, although the thought of reaching both places seemed totally unreal. Kingman is known as the 'Plough Capital of Kansas' and, suprisingly, the 'Cat Fish Capital of Kansas.'

GRAIN ELEVATOR AND SUNRISE

DAY 69—KINGMAN TO CUNNINGHAM—20 MILES (1,695 MILES)

The towns were now wider apart and the next one, Pratt, was 36 miles away. In 100 degrees I felt I should not attempt to walk that distance in a day, and on learning there was a small motel at Cunningham, I decided to stop there. The road was now very pleasant walking as I still followed Highway 54. After ten miles I reached the Kingman County State Park, with a lake on the right being avidly fished and a herd of buffalo on the left. The buffalo is now the state animal, being officially adopted in 1955, and this is one of the few surviving herds today. Two centuries ago the plains were covered by millions of buffalo which were the life support of the Plains Indians for food and clothing. In the middle of last century the 'White Hunters' came and killed indiscriminantly and slaughtered millions, often just for the tongue of the beast. Between 1868-1881, carbon companies paid out $2,500,000 for buffalo bones—estimated at 31,000,000 animals.

Cunningham was a small place, and at first the motel appeared closed, but I soon learnt the owners were also auctioneers and were holding an auction nearby. Going under the hammer were many 'British' memorabilia, including a red telephone kiosk and a 1956 Bentley for $16,000. From here onwards as I crossed the remainder of Kansas I would be slowly ascending to the Rockies in Colorado.

BUFFALO

DAY 70—CUNNINGHAM TO PRATT—20 MILES (1,715 MILES)

I was again walking just after 6.0a.m. to get a good few miles in before the heat began to slow me down. Kansas was the hottest place in America at the time with the fourth day in a row when it topped 104 degrees. After six hours of continuous walking I entered Pratt and immediately checked into a motel. Leaving my gear I walked into the town to purchase films and see the Homestead Museum.

Spies were obviously out, for, on buying some film, the sales assistant immediately contacted the local paper and asked if I would call by. I did, and related my story so far. The next day my photograph and story were on the front page of the Pratt Tribune—'Britain treks across U.S.'

I had already decided that I would try and remain incognito from now onwards, for I found the effort of the walk demanding all I had. Whilst I enjoyed the attention of the press and media, no one could really appreciate the strain I was under attempting such a major walk. I had ceased my radio reports back to England simply because I found it too emotional to do and had to psyche myself up before dialling. The walk was proving the hardest I had ever done and was already making my others pale into insignificance. Only in a few isolated places did I reveal what I was up to for the walk was starting to become 'beyond belief'.

Returning to the motel, I visited the Museum, and up a side street was suprised to see that someone had painted on the water towers, 'Hot and Cold.'

PRATT, HOT AND COLD

DAY 71—PRATT TO GREENSBURG—31 MILES (1,746 MILES)

As it had said in the paper, my destination for the day was Haviland; 21 miles. But the weather was cooler and, when I arrived there I decided to press on to Greensburg. I was partly urged on by the road signs that kept informing everyone that, 'Greensburg has the world's largest man-made well.' Walking in this area was slightly off-putting, for you could see miles ahead; often when I set out in the morning my destination could be seen. Standing out like ships in the prairies were the tall white grain elevators. It never ceased to amaze me that after 15 miles of walking they had not grown in size. In fact it wasn't until the final three miles did they suddenly increase in size.

Few cars ever stopped, but 8 miles from Greensburg a car headed towards me and stopped. The driver had seen me walking along and been to Greensburg for coke and beer, for he felt sure I needed a drink! He had cycled across America a few years ago and knew what I was experiencing, although he was taken aback that I was walking about the same distance each day as he had cycled. He was currently driving from coast to coast to a new job in Los Angeles. He had left Florida three days previously and expected to be in L.A. in a couple of days. The Pacific coast for me was about 3½ months away!

Before resting I had to see the hand-dug well. It was excavated in 1887 at a cost of $45,000 and served the town of Greensburg until 1932. The well measures 32 feet in diameter and is 109 feet deep. In the adjoining museum is another world beater—the largest pallasite meteorite (space wanderer). This was found on Ellis Peck farm east of Greensburg.

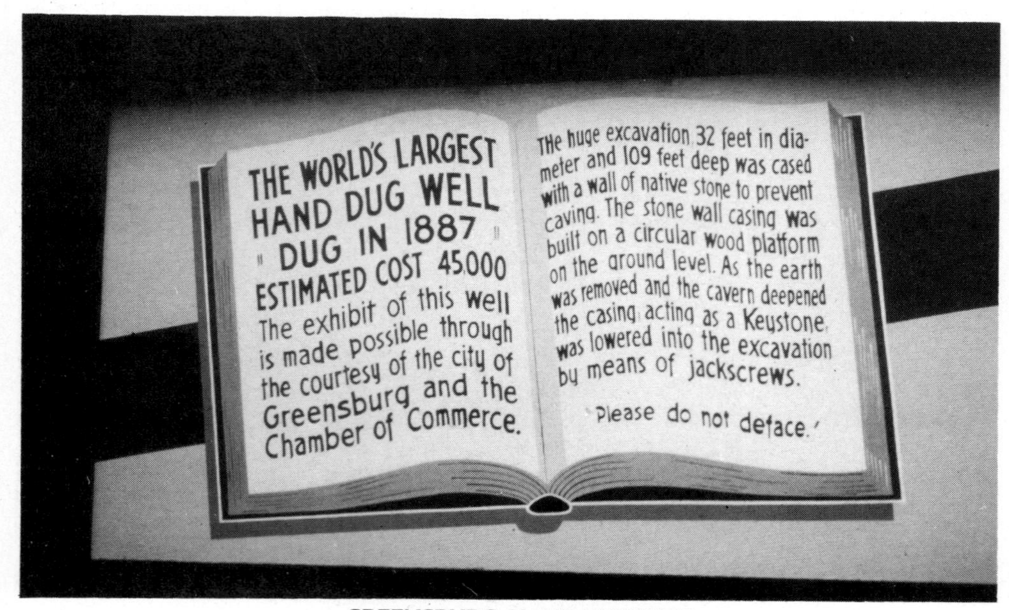

GREENSBURG, HAND DUG WELL

DAY 72—GREENSBURG TO BUCKLIN—21 MILES (1,767 MILES)

My last day on Highway 54, thankfully not as hot as of late but the humidity was increasing. First stop was in Mullinville, where I felt tired after yesterday's walk, and to boost my energy I drank half a gallon of milk! The fields were massive, often a mile long and very dry; even the river channels were dry. Keeping me company was the South Pacific railroad and the trains, often ¾ mile long, hooted and waved as they went past. The terrain was undulating which made a change, although the white grain elevator often shimmered like a mirage in the heat. Sun flowers grew beside the roadside.

Part way along the road I noticed the sign of a plane on the road; at first I thought the road was used as a runway, especially when I passed a two tier mail box the upper marked Air Mail. Later I was informed the signs were used by the police above monitoring a car's speed against the signs. I entered Bucklin feeling very tired, and even my feet seemed tired—looking at them they had become a little puffy. I checked into a motel and fell instantly asleep.

COWBOY MAIL BOX

DAY 73—BUCKLIN TO DODGE CITY—28 MILES (1,795 MILES)

Leaving Bucklin at dawn, just as the sun rose from behind a grain elevator, I headed north westerly towards Dodge City along Highway 154. Again it was hot, rising to 96 degrees, and at 8.0p.m. that evening it had only dropped to 90 degrees and at 10p.m. 85 degrees. The day was to prove one of the most memmorable of the whole walk, and resulted primarily from my decision not to do any research beforehand. Therefore what I came to was a surprise and meant one was eager to see 'round the corner.'

A little after the village of Ford,ten miles out, I crossed the Arkansas River which was dry and its bed could be traced a little to my right for the next few days. I could sense something was ahead as I passed old wooden buildings left to slowly decay, with windmill driven wells simply falling apart. Next I gained the Coronado Historical Park and sat in the shade. A plaque records Coronado's journey,who was a Spanish explorer, in 1540-41 from Mexico to North America searching for gold. He had just crossed the notorious Arkansas River, which was a far cry from the dry bed that exists today. The cross on the hill above the park records Coronado's mass after crossing the river—the first Christian service held west of the Mississippi in 1541. Close by was my first historical marker on the basic line of the Santa Fe Trail. The trail was a major route between 1822-1872 and for the next few days to Bent's Fort in Colorado, where it heads south, it would be keeping me company.

Already stimulated by these sights I gained Fort Dodge, and sat in the store and drank a quart of milk. The fort was built in 1865 and named after Major General Grenville M. Dodge. The fort was a base against the Plains Indians and close to a campsite on the Sante Fe Trail. The fort remained in use until 1882 and is now a State soldiers' home. A little further with Dodge City in sight, I entered huge cattle-fattening areas, with thousands of cattle being fatted before slaughtering. It all looked most gruesome with vast areas of cattle on one side of the road and a huge meat processing plant on the other. You could see an endless stream of cattle waiting in line to enter the building, with trucks at the other end ready to depart with packaged meat. There was also a constant flow of cattle trucks pouring along the road. I fell in line with a worker beside the road who told me they process enough meat in a day to feed 100,000 people!

BOOT HILL FRONTAGE

I pressed on feeling weary, as I had walked through the hottest part of the day to get here. Dodge City has an interesting history made famous by its gunfights. Established in 1872 it soon became known as the 'Cowboy Capital of the World' and 'The Wickedest Little City in America.' Perhaps its most significant title for me was, 'Where East meets West'. I had now crossed to the west. I felt a celebration was in order and stayed at the Lora Locke Hotel, built in the 1920's at a cost of $300,000. The famous have stayed here including Charles Lindberg, who flew in, and film stars like Errol Flynn and Olivia DeHavilland.

Although tired, I rushed out to explore the downtown area, walking along aptly-named streets, such as Wyatt Earp Street and Gunsmoke Street. My destination was Boot Hill Museum, where many of the early buildings of Dodge City are preserved, with characters playing the part of the early city life. I arrived just in time for the hourly gunfight and later the can-can girls. Between the two displays I visited the remains of Boot Hill Cemetery where many gunfighters were laid to rest—named Boot Hill for they were buried with their boots on! There were several amusing gravestones—see photographs.

Back at the hotel I ate my way through a rib eye steak before dashing to the pictures—not to see the movie, Dodge City, that was premiered here in 1939, but the Last Starfighter, which everyone was raving about. A strange end to a remarkable day.

BOOT HILL GRAVESTONE

BOOT HILL GRAVESTONE

DAY 74—DODGE CITY TO CIMARRON—20 MILES (1,815 MILES)

To my surprise I didn't wake up until 8.0a.m., but after a hotcake breakfast I was walking half an hour later. Thankfully it was cool at first, but the Kansas heat soon reached the mid 90's. Everywhere looked parched—the fields and river channels. Several stretches of the road bordered huge fields of corn overwhich swirled watering machines. Some were pivoted in the middle, and I looked across and saw a circular green area in the middle of dry brown area. As usual the white grain elevators stood out like beacons ahead, calling me on.

After a few miles I came to the large sign for the Santa Fe Trail tracks, said to preserve some of the finest remnants of the trail. Although I had seen pictures in Boot Hill Museum and reached the plaque on the site, I was still unsure which were the right ones, for it was difficult to differentiate between human and wagon tracks. In the end I photographed both.

I knew I wasn't walking well—the effort of yesterday and the excitement of all that I had seen had drained me. I reached Cimarron feeling tired. Watching the news later with the final buildup for the Los Angeles Olympic Games, it was interesting to learn that Americans this summer will consume 250 million gallons of ice cream!

LORA LOCKE HOTEL

DAY 75—CIMARRON TO GARDEN CITY—29 MILES (1,844 MILES)

I was up early chastising myself from having an easy day yesterday, but I could hear a strange noise. It was raining and hard, in fact 0.82′ fell and for awhile everything was awash with water. I waited until the rain eased and set off at the late hour of 10a.m. For the first hour I walked hard at my annoyance at such a late start. First stop was six miles out at Ingalls to visit the Santa Fe Trail museum. Cimarron was once an important crossing on the Trail, and the Cimarron Crossing Park has a replica of a covered wagon.

Fortunately the heat never rose above 80 degrees as cloud obscured the sun. The road was still long, and in the distance the grain elevators could be seen. I was now following Highway 50, passing through the hamlets of Charleston and Pierceville where the road left the Arkansas River and looped round the airport to Garden City. As I reached the eastern side I felt contented after such a long walk. That evening I sat entranced watching the opening ceremony of the 23rd Olympiad in Los Angeles. The ceremony was spectacular and very moving. I must admit I was very pro-American and seeing the teams enter the main stadium showed no emotion at the British team. When the American team entered in their stunning outfits, a lump came into my throat and I cried with emotion—'Go for it' I yelled.

SANTA FE TRAIL MARKER

DAY 76—GARDEN CITY TO LAKIN—27 MILES (1,871 MILES)

Although the population of Garden City is only 14,790, ten miles of walking was needed to cross through it. There was much to see as I walked through; apart from a large zoo it has the world's largest free concrete municipal swimming pool. It is so big in fact, that when opened as part of the celebrations, a power boat was brought in and someone water skied! The Windsor Hotel, which was built in 1886 and has a lobby three stories high, is referred to as 'The Waldorf of the Prairies.' A month before had been held the annual 3-I show—Industry, Irrigation and Implement—the largest in America. Also held at this time is the Beef Empire Days, featuring barrel racing, wild cow milking, carcass cattle show, and a Miss Beef Empire Days Contest. South of the city and well off my route is a 3,600 acre Buffalo Park State Game refuge, where the largest herd of buffalo in Kansas have their home.

I continued on Highway 50 to Holcomb and Deerfield. The whole area was extensively irrigated with waterchannels, canals and pipes, and the road ran between the tall corn. The sun beat down and my face soon became burnt as I failed yet again to put cream on or wear my hat. Fortunately there was a strong wind which gave some relief from the 90 degree heat. Beyond Deerfield I passed another milestone of the walk, entering Mountain time—England was now 7hrs ahead and, unlike my previous time zone, I had no difficulty in adjusting my watch immediately. I reached here at 4.0pm. really 3p.m. from now onwards.

I stopped in Lakin and that night noted in my log, 'although nearly 2,000 miles, my feet still complain and the rucksack still feels heavy!'

JOHN MERRILL AND MOUNTAIN STANDARD TIME

DAY 77—LAKIN TO SYRACUSE—
27 MILES (1,898 MILES)

I was walking by 6.30a.m. in a cool but cloudless day, still on Highway 50 and still following the line of the Sante Fe Trail. The day was to be my last full one in Kansas, and I felt quite sad for I had really enjoyed crossing this hot dry state. The temperatures had been coped with and, as if a parting shot today, it reached 98 degrees. The countryside was full of corn and large cattle fattening ranches and surprisingly hilly, although on the last hill it was off-putting to see Syracuse 12 miles ahead.

The day was full of surprises, and around noon a Deputy Sheriff pulled up and offered me breakfast at his home. We drove off the highway to the only house for miles and sat down to a delicious breakfast of hot cakes and bacon, despite the lunchtime hour! Rob proved an excellent host, with two lively dogs and a couple of tame racoons. They had hand-reared them and we found them curled up in a corner of the garden. An hour later, while Rob went to bed, his wife drove me back to the road before going into Garden City for the groceries.

Four hours later I entered Syracuse, and couldn't help but stay at the 'Ramble N Motel', it seemed too apt for my last night in Kansas. The owners were full of interest in my walk and the Syracuse Journal reporter called round for the story. Where I entered Kansas at Fort Scott I was 800 feet above sea level. As I crossed the State I had been slowly ascending. Syracuse was 3,250 feet above sea level.

SYRACUSE AND HIGHWAY 50

DAY 78—SYRACUSE TO HOLLY, COLORADO—21 MILES (1,919 MILES)

I set off at a brisk pace rather late as I had overslept. I knew I was leaving Kansas, and I felt sad letting my mind roll back to the crossing of the Flint Hills, Wichita and its downtown area, and of course Dodge City. It all seemed so long ago. I was still on Highway 50 and at Coolidge, my last place in Kansas, I called into the store and drank ½ gallon of milk; I walked well after that!

Before I knew it I had entered Colorado, the land of colour and mountains, although I couldn't see any. I took my obligatory photograph and visited the rest area, which was a stark contrast after so much dry brown earth, being lush green and with sprinklers watering the grass. The water faucet issued cool water—Rocky Mountain water? The road was now much wider, with wide shoulders for me to walk along. I had a decided spring in my step as I walked the final four miles to Holly—the Christmas city. I camped in the campground before celebrating with a steak. I watched a bit of the Olympics but soon drifted back to the tent and fell instantly asleep.

COLORADO STATE SIGN

COLORADO—THE CENTENNIAL STATE —Gateway to the Rocky Mountain West

CAPITAL—DENVER

POPULATION—(1980 CENSUS)—2,888,834

HIGHEST ELEVATION—MOUNT ELBERT, 14,433 FEET

LOWEST ELEVATION—HOLLY, 3,350 FEET

TOTAL AREA—8TH IN SIZE—104,247 SQUARE MILES

STATE BIRD—LARK BUNTING

STATE TREE—BLUE SPRUCE

STATE FLOWER—COLUMBINE

The 38th state admitted to the Union on August 1st 1876. A land of superlative scenery with 53 mountains over 14,000 feet. The Continental Divide, which separates the drainage to the Pacific Ocean and Atlantic Ocean, runs through the State. Colorado has the highest average elevation outside Alaska and is known as the 'Ski Country U.S.A.' Because of its abundance of campsites it is also known as the Camping Capital of America.

JOHN MERRILL ON THE SUMMIT OF UNCOMPAGRE PEAK

COLORADO

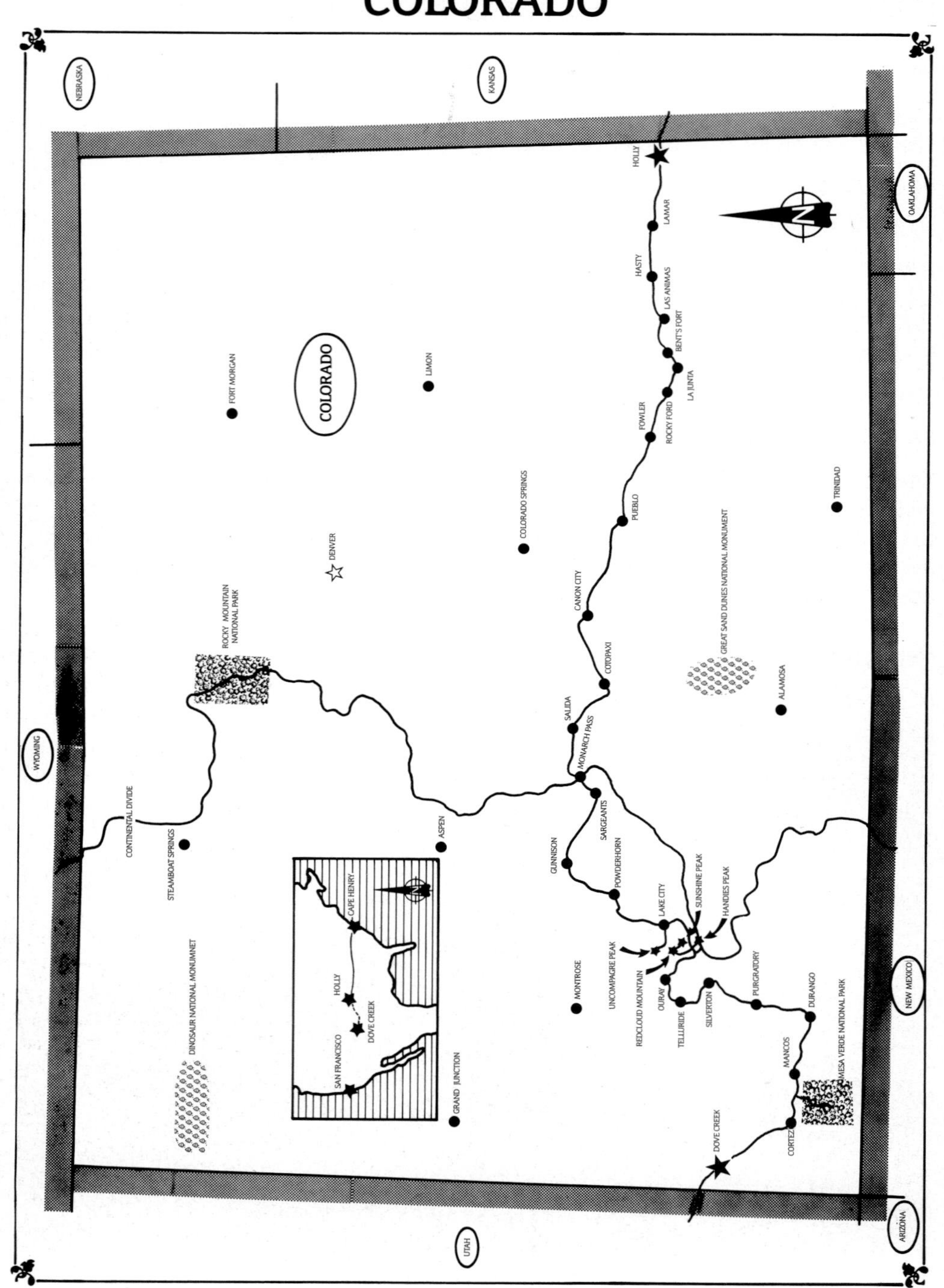
NEBRASKA
KANSAS
OAKLAHOMA
WYOMING
NEW MEXICO
ARIZONA
UTAH
COLORADO
HOLLY
LAMAR
HASTY
LAS ANIMAS
BENT'S FORT
LA JUNTA
ROCKY FORD
FOWLER
PUEBLO
CANON CITY
COTOPAXI
SALIDA
MONARCH PASS
SARGEANTS
GUNNISON
POWDERHORN
LAKE CITY
SUNSHINE PEAK
HANDIES PEAK
UNCOMPAGRE PEAK
REDCLOUD MOUNTAIN
OURAY
TELLURIDE
SILVERTON
PURGRATORY
DURANGO
MANCOS
MESA VERDE NATIONAL PARK
CORTEZ
DOVE CREEK
TRINIDAD
GREAT SAND DUNES NATIONAL MONUMENT
ALAMOSA
LIMON
FORT MORGAN
COLORADO SPRINGS
DENVER
ROCKY MOUNTAIN NATIONAL PARK
CONTINENTAL DIVIDE
STEAMBOAT SPRINGS
ASPEN
MONTROSE
GRAND JUNCTION
DINOSAUR NATIONAL MONUMNET
CAPE HENRY
HOLLY
DOVE CREEK
SAN FRANCISCO

DAY 79—HOLLY TO LAMAR—
28 MILES (1,947 MILES)

As if to celebrate my arrival in Colorado, I set off at 6.0a.m.—a new month, August, and a new state. I went without breakfast until I reached Granada after 2¾ hours walking, 11 miles away. Holly is the lowest point in Colorado at 3,350 feet and, although I did not know it then, I would ascend several mountains over 14,000 feet. I kept to my beloved Highway 50 which would eventually lead me to Canon City and the Rocky Mountains.

The heat of Kansas still operated in this part of Colorado, being dry and over 90 degrees. I saw many more sun flowers by the roadside here than I did in Kansas. Small yellow butterflies flew in profusion, and mostly corn was growing in the fields. Overhead an aircraft kept spraying the crops. A pungent smell of rotting undergrowth hung over the area and swarms of mosquitoes constantly attacked my bare arms and legs. I learnt later that a flash flood two weeks ago had caused the smell and awoken the mosquitoes.

I was walking well and passed through Carlton to reach Lamar. I really felt as though my fitness worries were now behind me and I was approaching my peak fitness. I had adjusted to road walking a lot, although this would soon change, and was setting a good pace. I wrote in my log that night, 'I feel fit, walking well—averaging 3½ miles per hour with 45 pounds on my back.'

Lamar is the county seat of Prowers County and part of the great plains area. Lamar is known as an 'all American City' and the Goose Hunting Capital of America. 500,000 acres of Prowers County is farmed, of which 100,000 acres is irrigated, producing $14 million worth of crops. Livestock production includes 75,000 head of cattle and 60,000 sheep raised annually. The weather is moderate with 15.8 inches of rain per year. The average temperature is 54.2 degrees all year and the sun shines out of the blue eastern Colorado sky 95% of the days each year!

CATTLE FATTENING

DAY 80—LAMAR TO McCLAVE—16 MILES (1,963 MILES)

My walking happiness of yesterday seemed short-lived for I felt unwell and was walking slowly. I stopped at the Big Timbered Museum only to find it closed. I ambled on to a KOA campground and drank a quart of milk. I felt slightly revived and pressed on, but on reaching Hud's Campground near McClave I called it a day. The tent was soon up and I fell asleep immediately for a couple of hours. I couldn't think what was wrong, unless the water melon I had eaten the night before had upset me.

I lay in the tent reading for four hours about the Scott and Amundsen race for the South Pole. I was not down in spirits, pleased that I had made the effort to walk a short distance. I reflected that in the past one of my rules has been to walk 2,000 miles within 80 days. I was a little short of that target but I had never walked so much in such high temperatures before, so I was more than satisfied.

HIGHWAY 50

DAY 81—McCLAVE TO LAS ANIMAS—22 MILES (1,985 MILES)

I awoke at 5.30a.m. feeling much better, and ate my way through four danish pastries and a pint of pure orange juice. The tent was soon down, and half an hour later I was on the tarmac once more. After six miles I reached Hasty and had another breakfast—2 eggs. hash browns, coffee and toast. I seemed to be making up for yesterday's lethargic walk. After 22 miles in 94 degrees I reached Las Animas and decided to stay, especially as they had a museum to explore.

Everyone was most helpful and full of interest in my walk. Las Animas is referred to as the 'Gateway to the Rockies' but I searched the horizon and could see nothing. A block south of the courthouse I reached the Kit Carson Museum housed in an adobe building built in 1940 to house German War prisoners from World War 11. Included was the County Jail built in 1876 with the replica of a scaffold opposite. The museum proprieter showed me pictures of hangings and he could still personally remember witnessing these events. Another building was a log cabin stage station built in 1860 and used on the Santa Fe Trail, whose line I was still following. The proprieter escorted me around. I was the only visitor all afternoon and he took delight in showing me the various rooms full of item's including a petrified dinosaur footprint. Before leaving he insisted I had Herzog's book on Annapurna to read.

That night I kept up to date with the happenings in the Olympics. The US were sweeping the board at all events. The gymnastic team was doing splendidly, with the star being Mary Lou Retton. Her face etched with determination made her a favourite with the media and public, who willed her to win the gold—she did with perfection.

SAGEBRUSH

DAY 82—LAS ANIMAS TO LA JUNTA—20 MILES (2,005 MILES)

While eating breakfast the waitress explained how Las Animas became to be so named, 'City of lost souls.' The city is named after the nearby Picketwire river, originally named by Spanish explorers in about 1594 as Rio de Las Animas Perdidas en Purgatorio—the river of lost souls in purgatory. I set off shortly after 6.0.a.m. still following the line of the Santa Fe Trail to Bent's Fort. The scenery was changing from flat to hilly prairie and for the first time I could see the faint outline of the Rockies, 80 miles away—two hours drive!—whilst I had the usual mid 90 degree heat to contend with, grasshoppers were constantly jumping on and off my legs, and both sand and deer flies were constantly biting me.

I followed the old highway, No 194, as this would take me away from the main roads and lead me to Bents Old Fort. Early afternoon I approached the fort, leaving my pack with a bewildered attendant. The fort, built in 1833/34 by Charles and William Bent and Ceran St Vrain, became a major staging and trading post on the Santa Fe Trail. The legendary Kit Carson was a hunter here, with land near Las Animas. The fort prospered and, to strengthen ties with the Cheyenne Indians, William Bent married Owl Woman, daughter of Gray Thunder, in 1837. Ten years later, with the growth of the west and Mexican Wars, the fort was finally abandoned in 1849 and believed to have been set alight.

The building was made from prairie soil with a mixture of straw and plain grass. Despite its simple construction it was an impressive fort. In the last decade the fort has been reconstructed by the National Park Service and is most tastefully done, illustrating amply life in the frontier days. Many locals dress up in the clothing of the time, with forges, fires and drying skins; it is little wonder that the site is now one of the major attractions of Colorado.

BENT'S FORT

I pressed on, sad to leave the Santa Fe Trail and headed on towards La Junta; another Spanish name meaning junction. Whilst the fort was a memorable place to see, the adventures of the day had only just begun. I passed a farm with a large abandoned van saying 'Peace'. Three miles later a truck pulled up and the driver offered me a place to camp at his farm—the one I had recently passed. The owner turned out to be Walt Cranson who had his own farm, had recently been an 'extra' an a film being made at the fort, and owned a bookshop in La Junta. I was made most welcome, and after a rest in the shade visited the city to see his 'bookstop' before going to a rodeo. Little was happening there, so we back tracked to the city to the Koshare Indian Museum.

Never having seen true Indian dancing I jumped at the chance to see a display. The kiva is made from logs and has a remarkable roof of logs placed in a spiralling formation using no nails. The 'Indian' dancers are scouts, and it is through their determination to keep alive the traditions of their past that every year about fifty performances are held. That night they danced around the room doing a variety of traditional dances, including one with live snakes, which I found alarming. They might be harmless ones, but holding them in one's mouth while dancing was not my idea of fun!

JOHN MERRILL AND PEACE SIGN

DAY 83—LA JUNTA TO ROCKY FORD—18 MILES (2,023 MILES)

Before leaving the Cransons, Walt rang a local reporter in Swink and she caught up with me later on the road. I was now back on Highway 50 passing through a largely water melon and pepper growing area. Rocky Ford is known as the Melon capital of the world. Loretta Scott caught up with me and drove me to her house for coffee and cake, while she interviewed and photographed me. Three days later a photograph and half page article appeared in the Pueble Chieftain, entitled—'Walking is career to Briton'.

An hour later I was back on the highway, not walking as well as I should. The illness I had suffered a couple of days ago was still plagueing me and now I had diarrhoea. The temperature too was high—100 degrees. Upon reaching Rocky Ford I checked into a motel and slept all afternoon, not even the thunderstorm mid-afternoon awoke me.

SWINK WATER TOWER

DAY 84—ROCKY FORD TO FOWLER—20 MILES (2,043 MILES)

The sleep had obviously done me good, for I felt much better and more my usual determined self. The storm had cleared the air and Colorado lived up to its saying—'we have the bluest skies!' Another saying is, that if it rains, wait ten minutes! Nine miles out I entered Manzanola, which was where I planned to stop the previous day. Fate seemed to have acted in my favour, as the motel was for sale. Flags were in profusion as it was Colorado day.

I pressed on to Fowler, getting there early afternoon. I was still slowly ascending, as Fowler was 4,341 feet above sea level. I was also pleased to learn that Durango in Colorado was 351 miles away and San Francisco was 1,370 miles—I was making progress, although I was not even halfway yet on my route. The Rockies too were increasing in size and were beginning to dominate the horizon. Like the previous day the weather started hot and sunny with a storm late afternoon. Pueblo was 34 miles away and nowhere to camp or stay inbetween. Tomorrow would be a hard day.

ROCKY MOUNTAIN VIEW

DAY 85—FOWLER TO BAXTER— 30 MILES (2,073 MILES)

The road was now getting busy as I began approaching Pueblo and its Interstate network. After 19 miles the highway became dual-laned but I ignored the significance for ahead getting bigger every mile were the Rockies. For the first time I could make out field patterns on their slopes. Ah, for cooler temperatures, I thought; it was again in the mid 90's.

I was pleased that I had overcome my stomach upset and was walking well although my feet were sore from the old socks. I decided to stock up with new ones ready for the mountains, in Pueblo. Feeling slightly tired I reached Baxter close to Pueblo Airport after ten hours of non stop walking. Seeing a motel I decided to halt. Just as well, half an hour later a storm blew up, with winds upto 60 m.p.h. and ⅜" diameter hailstones! There was no restaurant nearby so I bought a gallon of milk from a gas station and drank that for my evening meal!

ARKANSAS RIVER

DAY 86—BAXTER TO WEST PUEBLO—15 MILES (2,088 MILES)

I was up early feeling very hungry, and by 6.30a.m. was on Highway 50 walking to a restaurant. In fact it was six miles until I came to a Pancake House, and there I rather surprised the waitress with my appetite. Apart from the usual eggs, hash browns, coffee and toast, I also consumed three strawberry filled pancakes covered with whipped cream!

Fortified, I began my shopping spree ready for the mountains as I had very little clothing. First to the Post Office where a card and present were waiting from Sheila. Alas no letters, and my birthday was eleven days ahead. I called into a film store and stocked up with film. The owner was most interested in my walk and, pulling out a map of Colorado, suggested a route that I should take. My original plan had been to head north to the Rocky Mountain National Park, before heading down southwards through the state to Mesa Verde National Park. However, as it had taken longer to get here despite doing a longer mileage, I decided to head southwards, which he recommended. He said also that I would see the best of Colorado that way. He was right; the route I took over the Monarch Pass and southwards was a dream.

Excited at what I was about to do I rushed around the stores buying new socks, a T shirt—which I never wore—and a sweat shirt for warmth which I also never wore until California. I hunted around for guidebooks but found nothing. I went slightly mad and bought luxuries such as a new toothbrush, paste and hair shampoo! I continued on through the city, and, on the western side, seeing a Motel 6 and numerous restaurants nearby, decided to have an easy afternoon and study the maps and write a few postcards to let Sheila know all was well. The thought of food and restaurants was also most appealing. I also wanted to learn how the Olympics were going, and watched Carl Lewis win yet another medal. Daley Thompson was also doing well and seemed certain of a gold.

VIEW TO ROCKIES

DAY 87—WEST PUEBLO TO KOA—18 MILES (2,106 MILES)

I set off full of confidence with a bounding step—the mountains here I come—but I soon felt tired. The problem was the temperature; more than 90 degrees again. I had now come to the conclusion that, although I had adjusted to it, it was wearing me down and simply sapping my strength. When I reached the KOA campground in the middle of nowhere, I couldn't resist camping and resting. Just as well, for in the afternoon despite the weather forecast a storm moved in and rain lashed against the tent for a couple of hours. Late afternoon the sun came out, and Pike's Peak, 14,110 feet, just to the north of me, was snow covered.

I lay in the tent while the wind toyed with it, slowly drinking a gallon of milk and reading another 100 pages of Scott and Amundsen's book. To complete my mountain preparation I washed all my clothes.

ROYAL GORGE AND SUSPENSION BRIDGE

DAY 88— KOA TO ROYAL GEORGE CAMPGROUND— 26 MILES (2,132 MILES)

After drinking a quart of milk the tent was soon packed, and by 6.20a.m. I was walking on the dual-laned highway 50 to Canon City. The temperature was cooler and I was operating better. Couldn't find anywhere for breakfast but near Penrose was able to get a cup of coffee and a couple of cream-filled Tinkles bars. After five hours I began to wonder where Canon City was, when rounding a corner there it lay with a McDonald's sign flashing in the sun! I had now reached an elevation of 5,300 feet.

In the local bookshop I was at last able to buy maps and a guide to Southern Colorado. The photographs looked stunning. Seeing a cobbler I felt I should have my boots checked and resoled. He inspected them and said they would last another 1,000 miles! To fit new soles would take all afternoon. I couldn't wait that long. The mountains were here, their call was too strong. I was to regret this urge later.

Just as I was about to leave Canon City, who should be on the sidewalk but the film man from Pueblo. He wished me luck and I set off up the now small highway, first passing the State Penitentionary on my right. It was good to be walking uphill after so much flat, and I slipped into to top gear as the temperature dropped to 80 and I functioned more normally and stormed the hill. I was bursting with joy to be here in trees and high mountains—the crossing of Kansas was worth it for this. I checked into the campground and erected the tent beside a pine tree.

I suppose I should have rested, but I was on an emotional high. First I went to see Buckskin Joe, Boomtown, just down the road famed for its movie location where several famous films have been shot, including Cat Ballou and True Grit. I had arrived just in time to see the Sheriff have a shoot out with a couple of baddies. I went into a nearby restaurant and ate a buffalo steak, done real good! To end the day I took the little train to the view point over the Royal Gorge. The gorge is spanned by a bridge, 1,055 feet above the Arkansas River, and is the world's highest bridge.

ROAD TO CANON CITY

DAY 89—ROYAL GORGE TO COTOPAXI—26 MILES (2,158 MILES)

It was refreshing to wake up in cooler temperatures, and after half a mile I stopped for my usual large breakfast. First I had to descend to the Arkansas River which would be my companion for the next two days to Salida. As I descended the temperature rose, and for the next sixteen miles the gorge was a sun trap, back into the 90s and a burnt face! But the walking was enjoyable through the twisty gorge, often wary of vehicles coming round the tight corners. The river was full of white water sections, and a whole string of rafters floating their way down, yelling with glee.

My one regret is my dedication to walk, refusing to have time off as though I was cheating myself. I know in reality this is nonsense for I can over-do my singlemindedness. Seeing those rafters made me want to stop and join a descent party for the day, for I might never get the oppurtunity again. But I wouldn't stop, simply waving to them and photographing them like mad.

After almost ten hours and feeling tired from the sun, I entered Cotopaxi, named after the Ecuador peak. It had been a lucky day, for on the roadside I found a dollar note. There was another KOA campground here and I camped just above the river, having decided to join this excellent organisation and get discounts. That night I sat at my table and ate a tuna salad and drank another gallon of milk!

FLOATING THE RIVER

DAY 90—COTOPAXI TO SALIDA—26 MILES (2,184 MILES)

Again I was walking just after 6.0a.m., following a glass of milk for breakfast. The walking at first was impressive, through a narrow gorge, but after six miles the valley opened out with a high 10,000 foot ridge of mountains on my left—the San Isabel National Forest. I simply stared at their beauty, here at last were the mountains. At the Lazy J Campground I called into the restaurant for a late breakfast. Everyone enquired what I was doing. I casually mentioned I had so far walked from the Atlantic! I shouldn't have said that as I was trying to remain annoymous, but they all wished me well and shook me by the hand and refused to accept any payment for my meal.

By midday the weather had changed to black and ominous-looking. Seeing an aqueduct I sheltered underneath while a storm hurled hail and rain all around. An hour later it eased off but remained dull for the afternoon. Now back into cooler conditions, I began a routine as my fitness began to emerge. As a basic rule I was completing ten miles by 10a.m. and twenty miles by 2.0p.m.

Mid-afternoon I entered Salida (7,300 feet) and decided to stay at a motel, so that I could watch the final day of the Olympics. I was given a free ticket for a swim in Salida's hot springs, but didn't feel like walking another mile. The marathon was being run, and much to everyone's amazement Portugal won. The final closing ceremony was again a masterpiece of organisation and precision, and again a lump came in my throat as the US team entered the arena. The fireworks display concluded the Games, which were the most successful for America and had made a handsome profit.

RIVER NEAR SALIDA

DAY 91—SALIDA TO MONARCH SKI RESORT 19 MILES (2,203 MILES)

I needn't have set off so early as it was no longer necessary to 'beat the heat', but my routine was hard to get out of and I was walking by 6.15a.m. The temperature never rose more than 75 degrees. First it was through Poncho Springs on Highway 50 before entering the San Isabel National Forest and Howard County. A sign detailed the fact that Howard County was the home of ' 450 nice people' and, in bold letters, 'a few old soreheads!'

High mountains were now all around, and the road began its ascent to the Monarch Pass. I revelled in the thought of high mountains and views after the flatlands. Reaching a KOA I was tempted to stay but felt I should press on, and the owner recommended me to the Monarch Inn. I walked on, after downing a quart of milk. I was in no rush, just absorbing the scene—mountains, aspen trees and humming birds. I was also slightly worried about how I would perform at altitude and preferred to acclimatise slowly. I needn't have worried—I was so fit.

The walking was unreal after so long in the plains and heat of eastern America, that I simply stared at the trees, jumped at the squeak of a chipmunk and thrilled at the sight of a butterfly. I passed the sign of the Colorado Trail but over the next few days could find nothing about it. At 10,000ft I entered Monarch and checked in. This too seemed unreal, being in a ski resort; the experience was mind blowing when I lay in a jaccuzzi in the open at 10,000 feet! It seemed the Colorado pattern as a storm passed through in the afternoon with heavy rain.

TOWARDS MONARCH PASS

DAY 92—MONARCH SKI RESORT TO MONARCH VALLEY RANCH CAMPGROUND 20 MILES (2,223 MILES)

I left at 7.0a.m., and although it was only 48 degrees I just had my shorts and T shirt on. I was still worried about acclimatisation for after 10,500 feet the thinner air begins to sap one's strength. But, I had no ill effects and leaped up the road to the top of the Monarch Pass, 11,312 feet. I was jubilant, but couldn't find anyone to photogragh me beside the sign. Here was the Continental Divide which divides the continent—rain falling on the eastern side (Monarch) will drain into the Atlantic and on the western side—THE PACIFIC. It was an important moment for me, especially when I was informed that San Francisco was only 1,175 miles away!

To celebrate I left the pack at the base station and took the cable car to the crest of the Divide at 12,000 feet—the ride frightened me looking down the steep slopes. From the top the view was magnificent with 13,000 and 14,000 foot mountains galore. The camera worked overtime, and at that point I didn't appreciate how involved I would become in these high mountains. Back at the pass a group of cyclists had cycled up and were being photographed at the sign. They obligingly took my photograph, and with a definite spring in my step I began descending the highway (50) and entering Gunnison National Forest.

I planned to reach Gunnison the next day, 40 miles away, and hoped to reach a campground 12 miles away today in readiness. The mountains were short lived as I descended 4,000 feet back into lower country and back into heat. In the village of Sargeants I couldn't resist a hamburger and toyed with the idea of stocking up with food for the campsite, but the advert for the campground stated that it had a store, so I abstained. Five miles later I entered th campground and camped free! Although open the long winter had delayed the building of all the facilities. The owner drove me back to Sargeants for food!

JOHN MERRILL ON THE SUMMIT OF MONARCH PASS HIGHWAY

DAY 93—
MONARCH VALLEY TO GUNNISON—
28 MILES (2,251 MILES)

A quart of milk served as breakfast before packing up the tent in decidedly cool weather—42 degrees. For the first time for months I even had to wear my wind-jacket. The walking was most pleasant close to the Tomichi Creek and through grassland along a water eroded valley, hovering around the 8,000 foot mark. After 18 miles I reached Parlin and drank another quart of milk. It was also a relief to be inside, for big deer flies were being a constant nuisance, biting chunks out of me if I wasn't looking.

Beyond Parlin the sun came out and the air soon warmed up, but entering Gunnison the sky darkened and a storm passed through. I checked into a motel and on my way to eat saw a bookshop and purchased maps and a guide to Hiking Trails of Southwestern Colorado. At last I could plan to do something as I passed through the area; the call of the high mountains was too strong. Back in the motel I spread the map out and decided to walk to Lake City before climbing a few 14,000 mountains in that locality. My birthday was soon approaching and one of my rules is to climb a high mountain to celebrate.

NR MONARCH PASS

DAY 94—GUNNISON TO POWDERHORN—28 MILES (2,279 MILES)

Gunnison is the centre for a very attractive area, with old mining ghost towns, lakes which are part of the Curecanti National Recreation Area and the famed Black Canyon of Gunnison National Monument. Alas I couldn't do everything and had to content myself by walking past Beaver Creek and around part of the Iola Basin where numerous people were fishing, before leaving Highway 50 and following 149 southwards to Lake City.

The road began to climb and it became hotter but I still refused to carry water. My throat soon became parched but I felt convinced I would reach water soon. Instead the road climbed and the countryside was dry. After five hours it was a relief to descend to the Cebolla Creek near Powderhorn. I was feeling awful by this time and just immersed myself in the water and drank and drank the cool water. Refreshed I carried on and two hours later just sat by the road as a car pulled up. The owner offered to take me to Lake City and a campground. I hadn't the heart to refuse and so began one of the most amazing twenty four hours of the walk.

The camp was full of Texans with huge trailers. All were extremely friendly,somewhat amused to find a camper in their midst. In the evening I purchased a day pack before joining a group of Texans around a log fire. Apparently they were part of an annual migration for they come here every May and stay for four months to escape the heat. A lot of tall stories floated around, and as my companion commented I was hearing a lot of Texas lies!

I was tired but elated to be here by a twist of fate. I should have gone back to where I was given a lift but decided to do that two days ahead, for looking in the guide were three 14,000 foot mountains within easy reach. With a day pack and leaving the tent and gear I could ascend Uncompahgre Peak, 14,309 feet, from Lake City, and this I resoloved to do the next day. The following day I would return to the road and complete the section into Lake City and continue on up the valley to another campground. From there on my birthday I would climb two 14,000 foot peaks. The plan looked exciting; would the weather hold?

IOLA BASIN

DAY 95— LAKE CITY TO UNCOMPAHGRE PEAK AND BACK—24 MILES (2,303 MILES)

I left at 6.15a.m. without breakfast and just had a couple of Snickers bars and some M & M's in my pack. First it was along the track beside Henson Creek for six miles before turning and ascending the jeep trail up Nellie Creek to the trailhead at 11,000 feet. Without a load I was walking well and in devastating form, able to push myself at will. Just as I neared the trailhead a couple of jeeps passed full of climbers. I soon caught them up and beat them to the summit! It had taken six hours of walking. The view was staggering over ridge and mountain as far as the eye could see. There were still large areas of snow left and in fact August is the only month when the high mountains are truly accessible. Early September sees the return of the snows. I was there at the right time.

After photographing myself by the cairn and writing in the log in the cairn I descended at speed fearing being caught in a storm, but none came. Nearing the trailhead I passed several clumps of columbines which stood out serenely from the stark countryside. Back on the trail I descended back into the woodland and past magnificent stands of Aspen trees, and after ten hours was back in Lake City, before the jeep teams! I had stunned the locals by doing the 24 mile return walk in ten hours which includes 6,000 feet of ascent and descent. I couldn't help letting my mind roll back to Cape Henry where I looked unfit, white and overweight! My decision not to train had been correct; I had reached the best part in perfect condition.

Back in the River Fork campground, news of my return spread like wildfire. I sat around the log fire listening to more Texas lies and becoming friends with several of the group; several of whom I still correspond with, such as Babs Bibbitt of Hamilton, Texas. That night I wrote simply in my log—'truly a great day'.

UNCOMPAGRE PEAK SUMMIT

DAY 96—POWDERHORN TO CASTLE LAKES CAMPGROUND—28 MILES (2,331 MILES)

Late start following heavy storm during the night, as I wanted to dry my tent before starting. I was soon returned to the road near Powderhorn, where I had been picked up two days before. With the pack on my back I set off along the road feeling slightly strange being in familiar area and with the weight on my shoulders. However I was in good spirits and enjoyed the walk close to the Lake Fork Gunnison River, which was being regularly fished. The scenery was dramatic as the road passed through an interesting gorge. On the way passing through 'The Gates', all that remains of a natural dam that formed a lake, as Lake City's name suggests. The area a hundred years ago was booming with silver and gold mines. There are several ghost towns in the area, some I would soon be seeing.

Beyond Lake City I almost encircled Lake San Cristobal, the second largest natural lake in Colorado, and extremely beautiful being surrounded by high mountains and attractive forest. I turned off and followed the Cinnamon Pass Road for Castle Lakes Campground. The owners, Dick and Mary Lee Cooper, gave me a warm welcome and allocated me a delightful site overlooking the lake. I mentioned I was pleased to be there for the next day was my birthday and I planned to climb the two 14,000 foot mountains—Sunshine Peak and Redcloud Mountain in the morning to celebrate! They wished me well and asked if I would join the 'all you can eat hamburger party' that night. I agreed.

Two hours later I went to the main room for the hamburgers and was just about to get one, when Mary Lee came out with a chocolate coated cake with five candles. Everyone sang Happy Birthday, although a day early. I was very embarrassed and didn't know what to do and was deeply touched by their generosity. Later I joined my next door neighbours, Collette and Claude from Texas—where else—for sherry and peaches and cream.

LAKE CITY AREA

DAY 97—
REDCLOUD AND SUNSHINE PEAK—
20 MILES (2,351 MILES)

My 41st birthday! I left at 6.30a.m. and followed the jeep trail up the valley for six miles, through absorbing scenery of deep valleys, forest and high mountains. At Silver Creek I turned off onto a faint trail and began the ascent of Redcloud Peak (14,034 feet). There were still several large patches of snow in the creek bottom and moving out into open country I disturbed a brown bear; the only one I saw on the whole walk. The ascent seemed to take a long time, and perhaps the effort of the last few days was starting to assert itself. However, I was soon on the summit in cloudy dull weather, wearing just shorts and a T-shirt. The weather in the distance looked ominous and a storm was erupting over Uncompahgre Peak.

I was unsure what to do, but with Sunshine Mountain (14,018 feet) a mile and a half away, it seemed a shame not climb it. I decided to chance it and run! Twenty minutes later I was on the summit and the storm had gone in the opposite direction! On reflection I must have been mad running at 14,000 feet at the tender age of 41 but I felt no ill effects, in fact I was full of energy. Rather than retrace my steps I plunged straight down the mountain, descending very rapidly a 2,000 foot scree slope. By early afternoon I was back at the jeep road and given a lift back to the campsite.

I was elated after climbing two peaks—5,000 feet of ascent. I quickly rang Sheila to let her know my current position and was amazed to get through straight away from my remote location, a nice birthday suprise. I sat outside and watched the humming birds zooming past my red socks, including a particularly attractive Ruby Throat. My Texan neighbours cooked a special chicken dinner and I pulled out of the rucksack a bottle of Californian rose I had purchased in Lake City the day before on my way there. Again, 'a truly exceptional day (birthday).'

JOHN MERRILL ON SUNRISE MOUNTAIN

DAY 98—HANDIES PEAK (14,048 FEET)—15 MILES (2,366 MILES)

A storm during the night had soaked the tent but the morning brought bright warm sun. I set off just after 6.0a.m. to climb my fourth 14,000 ft peak on the other side of the valley to the previous day. Dick Cooper saw me and insisted on driving me up to the trailhead. The trail was defined at first but in the forest I simply lost its line and emerged into open country at a cairn.The route was obvious close to Grizzly Glutch, but no trail signs on the ground as I gradually ascended up the high valley beneath the mountain wall. The view behind became spectacular over to Redcloud and Sunshine Peak.

A quick scramble up some rocks brought me to the summit ridge which I followed to the summit cairn. The view from here was even more impressive with the American Basin and Sloan Lake below dramatically framed by ominous black clouds. A few photographs and it was time to descend quickly as the thunder rolled. I descended towards Sloan Lake and sheltered at some rocks while it thundered and torrential rain streamed down. An hour later it was bright sun and the ground steamed away. The American Basin is famed for its wild flowers and the whole area was dotted with columbines. Many said it was the best in the area, but I was to see even better displays over the next few days.

Back at the jeep trail Dick Cooper was waiting; it was not pre-arranged, he just simply decided he had enough time to collect me, a most generous act. Back at the camp I relaxed by the lake watching the humming birds while reflecting on the day's climb and seeing squirrels, ground squirrels, coonies and chipmunks. I felt sad for it had been a wonderful few days here, but tomorrow I would put the pack on once more and continue my now devious route to the Pacific. I was awoken from my thoughts by Claude who announced tea was ready! They had been down to Lake City and bought a bottle of white wine and were cooking trout covered with almonds. The result was mouth watering and a delightful end to my stay here.

THE AMERICAN BASIN

DAY 99—CASTLE LAKES TO OURAY—18 MILES (2,384 MILES)

With heavy heart I called at the office to see Dick and Mary Lee, for I had had a wonderful stay here, quite unpremeditated. When I came to pay the bill, Dick just tore it up and said,'its been a pleasure having you stay'. He was really too kind and insisted on driving me up the jeep trail to where I had already walked to. We bade farewell, 'come back and see us sometime' he called. I hope to do so some day, perhaps on my walk along the Continental Divide in a couple of years time.

Back with my load my pace dropped to a steady one as I began ascending Cinnamon Pass over 13,000 feet. It was slightly off putting to sweat your way to the top of the pass only to be overtaken by a jeep party! Descending the other side I reached Animas Fork, a gold mining ghost town. The place was swarming with jeeps and I pressed on northwards to reach Ouray. I could have headed southwards to Silverton, 12 miles away, but I had fallen in love with the area and wanted to prolong my stay as much as possible. Besides, I could reach Silverton by doing a three day walk over several more high passes and that idea appealed very strongly.

After descending Bear Creek in the usual afternoon storm, I looked down on Ouray, known as the Switzerland of America. The location was particularly attractive with high mountains circling the area with the city laid out before me in a deep bowl.It is also known as the Jeep Capital of the World and with more than 800 miles of jeep trails in the area, it is little wonder the area is so popular—you don't have to walk to see the wonders of nature, a thrilling drive takes you there!

Ouray was a favourite camping place for Indians and is named after a Ute Chieftain. White men first came here in the 1870's, and its beauty and mining prospects soon brought it to the attention of all. Old mines litter the area, and linking Ouray and Silverton is the famous 'million dollar highway.' In 1923 the first five miles from Ouray cost a million dollars and was considered a 'foolish expense'.

OURAY

DAY 100—OURAY TO TELLURIDE—20 MILES (2,404 MILES)

My boots were now causing me concern; a blister had developed yesterday and they were slowly collapsing. I should have stopped at Canon City! However, I set off full of confidence and followed the road to Camp Bird, where the famous Hope Diamond was found, launching Evelyn Walsh McLean into Washington society. The climb to here had been steep but the ascent now became much steeper and longer to the top of the Imogene Pass, 13,114 feet. The basins were full of wild flowers and the final section was snow covered. Fortunately there was a ruined hut on the pass and I reached it just in time as a storm came in and it hailed hard.

COLUMBINES

I had more pressing problems; my right boot sole was falling off! I tied a spare boot lace around it and set off down towards Telluride, hoping for an outdoor store. First I came to the ruins of Tomboy mine which was once a huge and busy complex with 2,000 people working and was complete with supermarket, tennis courts and bowling alley. A little further and I saw Telluride for the first time; it was heaven. The setting was stunning with Bridal Veil Falls at the head of the valley and high mountains around. I descended in earnest hoping to get there before the stores closed. I arrived at 5.0p.m. and checked into the Youth Hostel—Oak Street Inn. A mushroom conference was in progress with the lobby floor strewn with more than 100 different mushrooms to 'try'!

There were three outdoor stores. The first two had no boots at all my size. The last one, Olympic Sports, had, but they cost $160! I was in a quandary. I tried them on and they felt perfect, by far the best I had ever seen. Having explained why I needed them the owner said I could have them for $79 as I had walked so far! He obligingly stuck the sole back on the old pair and I resolved to carry both pairs, switching from new to old over the next few days as the new pair were broken in. I headed back to the hostel just in time to grab my camera and photograph the finest rainbow I have ever seen—perhaps an omen.

RAINBOW, TELLURIDE

An hour later I sat in Floradora's Saloon and had a steak. Telluride is a beautiful place rich in history and now a famous ski resort. Of all the places I passed through, this was the only place I wanted to live, but on learning the house prices decided I couldn't afford to! The town was first settled in 1875 and ten years later with a population of 3,000 was part of the silver boom. Following the silver crash in 1893 the gold boom took over, but this too eventually declined and by 1929 the population was down to 512. Mining continued here until 1978 and the town is now Colorado's 'festival capital'. The downtown area is full of old buildings and has been preserved. Butch Cassidy robbed his first bank here in 1889 and in preparation practised several times his high speed getaway before the robbery!

DAY 101—TELLURIDE TO SILVERTON—22 MILES (2,426 MILES)

I set off in my new boots and eventually wore them for 4½ hours before my feet began to complain and I switched back to the old pair. My route was spectacular up the switchback trail beneath the Bridal Veil Falls, which fall 365 feet and are the highest falls in Colorado. The view back to Telluride and its valley was breathtaking; I was sorry to leave. Telluride is ofen refered to as—'to-hell-you-ride'—which seems unfair for it is more like heaven. Below were the remains of one of the mines—this area has produced $350,000,000 in ore. Perched at the top of the falls is the abandoned building of the Smuggler-Union hydro-electric power plant, now on the National Register of Historic Places.

The trail with its numerous switchbacks is still jeepable, but not used often because the bends are so acute, most jeeps overturn. As a result I had the area to myself and gradually climbed in solitude to the summit of Black Bear Pass. I was now moving out of the mountains and I felt slightly sad, for the last six days had been remarkable walking. I descended to the million dollar highway near Red Mountain Pass. I avoided the road as much as possible and descended to Silverton.

Silverton the 'Mining Town that Never Quit', was originally a mining camp, but in 1874, because, 'There's silver by the ton in those mountains', it was changed to Silverton. Mining is still continued in the area, and walking through the town is like being transformed back to the mining days. The period buildings retain its image. I checked into the Youth Hostel in the Teller House on Greene Street, before walking around to see the famous and notorious Blair Street. Rather like walking along a movie set with wooden buildings and sidewalks, wide dirt road and saloons on either side. I went into the Bent Elbow built in 1905 for a meal. The room was massive, and an elderly woman played non-stop on an old piano. Everyone approved and kept visiting her with a dollar for her to play their favourite tune. Blair Street earned its reputation from the many saloons and brothels that bordered the street; one had a plaque recording that there was a 'Madam' here until 1947.

BRIDAL VEIL FALLS AND SWITCHBACK TRAIL

DAY 102—
SILVERTON TO PURGRATORY SKI AREA—
28 MILES (2,454 MILES)

Today Silverton has a population of 850 and lies surrounded by the San Juan mountains at 9,318 feet. The average growing season is only 14 days and the average snowfall is 165 inches. The temperature at night is rarely above freezing any night of the year. As if to illustrate my point, when I set off it was only 42 degrees. I was now heading due south to Durango close to the New Mexico border. It was back to road walking following Highway 550. Linking Silverton and Durango is the famous narrow gauge Silverton Railway which I would see the next day puffing its way to Silverton.

My route took me into the Weminuche Wilderness and over the Molas and Coal Passes. Alas my feet were complaining, and after 2½ hours I had to revert to the old boots as blisters were developing. With the old ones on my feet I soon settled down and reached Purgratory feeling a little tired. The inn was full and I was given a lift to Durango where I stayed in the Youth Hostel—the last one on my route. Finding a film store I left five films to be processed and paid for them to be sent on to England. Amazingly I never lost a single slide or film from the walk.

Seeing an Italian restaurant I went for a lasagne. At the next table were a couple of attractive women—Cindy and Starr—who were curious about my tan. I am afraid I bored the pants off them by spending three hours telling them about the walk! It also transpired that they were staying at the hostel as well. During the conversation the people at the next table were also listnening to my story. When they got up to leave the gentleman came across and gave me his business card. He had written on it, 'If your journey passes through Cortez you are most welcome to stay and have a meal on me.' He was the owner of the Best Western Inn there and it was on my route!

SILVERTON

DAY 103—PURGRATORY TO DURANGO—22 MILES (2,476 MILES)

Walking out of Durango hoping to get a lift back to Purgratory ski area, a jeep pulled up and I was amazed to see the Duke family, one of the Texans I had met in Lake City. We went off for breakfast and I devoured three strawberry filled pancakes. They were visiting the area and happily drove me back to Purgratory. There I set off back to Durango wearing the old pair of boots, as my feet were still a little tender from wearing the new ones.

Later the Durango/Silverton train came puffing along on its four hour journey. The line was completed in 1882 and it is estimated that $300,000,000 worth of ore has been shipped along the route since then. Today the train is the only 100% coal-fired, narrow gauge railroad in the United States, and its 1880's carriages were full of people making the day return trip.

Durango is quite large with a population over 11,000 and is a popular vacation stop. I was worried about my new boots, and finding a store purchased a bottle of neatsfoot oil to soften the leather. I felt new socks would also help cushion my feet and I bought two pairs, throwing my old ones away. One pair of red ones had lasted all the way from Virginia Beach. I stayed again at the hostel, and at the movie theatre three blocks away the film 'Ghostbusters' was on. The film had caught everyone's attention and Ghostbuster T shirts and stickers were everywhere. I succumbed to the power of advertising and surprised myself at enjoying the film. One of the momentoes of the walk is the film's soundtrack, and when it opened in Britain after my return I took Sheila along to see it.

SILVERTON/DURANGO TRAIN

DAY 104—DURANGO TO MANCOS—29 MILES (2,505 MILES)

After calling in at a McDonalds for breakfast I headed westwards once more along Highway 160, wearing my new boots. After four hours my feet were decidedly sore and blisters were developing on my heels. Stopping at a gas station I switched to my old boots and put on new socks, throwing the old pairs away. My feet settled down and I enjoyed the walk skirting the western edge of the San Juan National Forest. The day proved particularly attractive with clear blue skies exposing the mountains with cyrstal clear sharpness and a pleasant 75 degrees.

I was awoken from my stupor by a jeep pulling up beside me; it was the Duke family again! They, like me, were heading for Mesa Verde National Park. Again they wished me well and stocked me up with apples and plums. Finding a rest area a mile later, I sat in the shade and ate my way through the fruit with the help of some friendly chipmunks. I pushed onto Mancus as I would be nicely placed to get to Mesa Verde tomorrow. I felt tired but elated at having now walked more than 2,500 miles.

THE WETHERALL MESA

DAY 105—MANCOS TO MESA VERDE—18 MILES (2,523 MILES)

I was back on the highway shortly after dawn, being eager to get to the National Park. I wore my old boots as I felt I should let my feet recover from yesterday's effort. I had hoped to camp at the campsite close to the highway, but as there was no store decided to walk into National Park and camp at the Morefield Campground, complete with store, showers and laundamat! It meant walking up the hill to it and I would have to retrace my steps later, but the ascent provided distant views over the Mancos valley.

I knew nothing about the National Park, but I soon learnt I had come to one of the most absorbing areas of America. I hitched a lift and was just in time to catch the bus and tour of the Wetherill Mesa, which although known to the Indians was not discovered by white man until 1891. Mesa Verde, which is Spanish for 'green table', was first settled by the Anasazi Indians in 550. They were expert basketmakers and lived on the top of the mesa in pithouses. 200 hundred years later their houses were built above the ground with walls of poles and mud and were known as Pueblos—village dwellers. By the year 1000 they were expert at stone masonry and pottery.

Mesa country is table top with river valleys exposing a rock escarpment often with high shallow caves. Some were used to live in but the majority lived on the mesa. About 800 AD the Anasazi moved from the mesa to the cliff alcoves and built dwellings that have since become world famous. Why they moved is still not understood, nor too is the reason why they suddenly left in 1300, but it is thought to be because of a twenty-year-long drought in the area. The cliff dwellings range from one building to the largest, the Cliff Palace, with over 200 rooms.

The Wetherill Mesa is believed to have accommodated between 1,000 and 2,000 Anasazi. Anasazi is a Navajo Indian word meaning, ancient ones. Excavations have revealed check dams and terraces, with the mesa top cultivated for corn, squash, beans, with an annual precipitation of 18 inches. Excavations began in 1891 and John Wetherill often acted as guide to parties from neaby Mancos. I was to see samples of the pottery and tools later in the museum. I found the exploring of the buildings, seeing the Kivas—ceremonial rooms underground—and petroglyphs absolutely fascinating.

Mesa Verde is the only National Park in America to safeguard antiquities and was formed in 1906. Although I was to see three cliff dwellings there have now been more than 800 located and more than 3,000 mesa top habitations.

MESA VERDE COUNTRY

DAY 106—MESA VERDE TO CORTEZ—18 MILES (2,541 MILES)

Back to my new boots today, and I wore them all day! The couple camping next to me gave me a lift to the museum area and at the Ranger's office I collected some mail—several birthday cards and three letters from Sheila. Emotionally I was at six's and seven's for an hour after reading the contents. To take my mind off things I first explored the Cliff Palace, by far the biggest group of dwellings. I marvelled at how the Indians would ascend and descend to their homes via hand and toe holes in the sheer rock walls, unlike the tarmaced paths we follow today.

Later I joined a guided party to the Spruce Tree House. This was the most adventurous to get to, involving a thirty foot ladder climb. The Ranger said she had not lost anybody yet! After exploring the rooms and kivas the ascent was spectacular across the rock wall with a 600 foot drop. I would have liked to have stayed longer but dedication to the walk made me itchy to continue. I returned to the campsite and packed the gear, descended the road to Highway 160 and turned left to Cortez.

A little way along the road and ahead could be seen the Sleeping Ute. An impressive mountain whose outline was just like a sleeping Indian, with head, folded arms, knees and toes. The roadside was lined with sunflowers, and with 90 degrees heat I felt I was back in Kansas. Two hours later I entered Cortez and looked for the Best Western Motel and checked in after showing my card, given to me in Durango. I was made most welcome and given reduced rates and a meal free in the Pony Express restaurant. Cortez dates from 1886 and is Spanish in origin but Hernando Cortez never came here. Lying to the southwest is the Four Corners, the only place in America where four states meet.

I was slightly torn where to go from here—Monument Valley was appealing and could be seen from Mesa Verde, but by taking this southern route I would miss several National Parks in Utah and decided that was my best route and in keeping with what I planned. I wrote to Sheila that night and looked forward to heading north westerly in the morning towards Utah.

OLD AND NEW BOOTS

DAY 107—CORTEZ TO DOVE CREEK—30 MILES (2,571 MILES)

Cortez is the county seat of Montezuma County which has an area of 2,097 square miles—more than the state of Maryland on the eastern side! After thanking the receptionist for my enjoyable stay, I headed out of Cortez on Highway 666. I was still wearing the new boots and, as the day progressed, was impressed how they were settling down, although my feet were a little sore.

I was now back to farming country as I walked through Yellow Jacket, Pleasant View and Cahone to Dove Creek, the latter being the 'Pinto Bean Capital of the world!' I did not intend walking so far especially in the heat—95 degrees again—but there was nowhere to stay and no campgrounds until a motel in Dove Creek. On the way I passed a monument to some Franciscans who in 1776 were lost in nearby Delores Canyon trying to find a way to the Spanish Mission in Monterey in California.

I felt sad that night knowing Colorado was now crossed; an amazing experience of heat and high mountains. Six miles—two hours—walking tomorrow would bring me to Utah. What, I wondered, would that be like?

THE CLIFF PALACE

UTAH

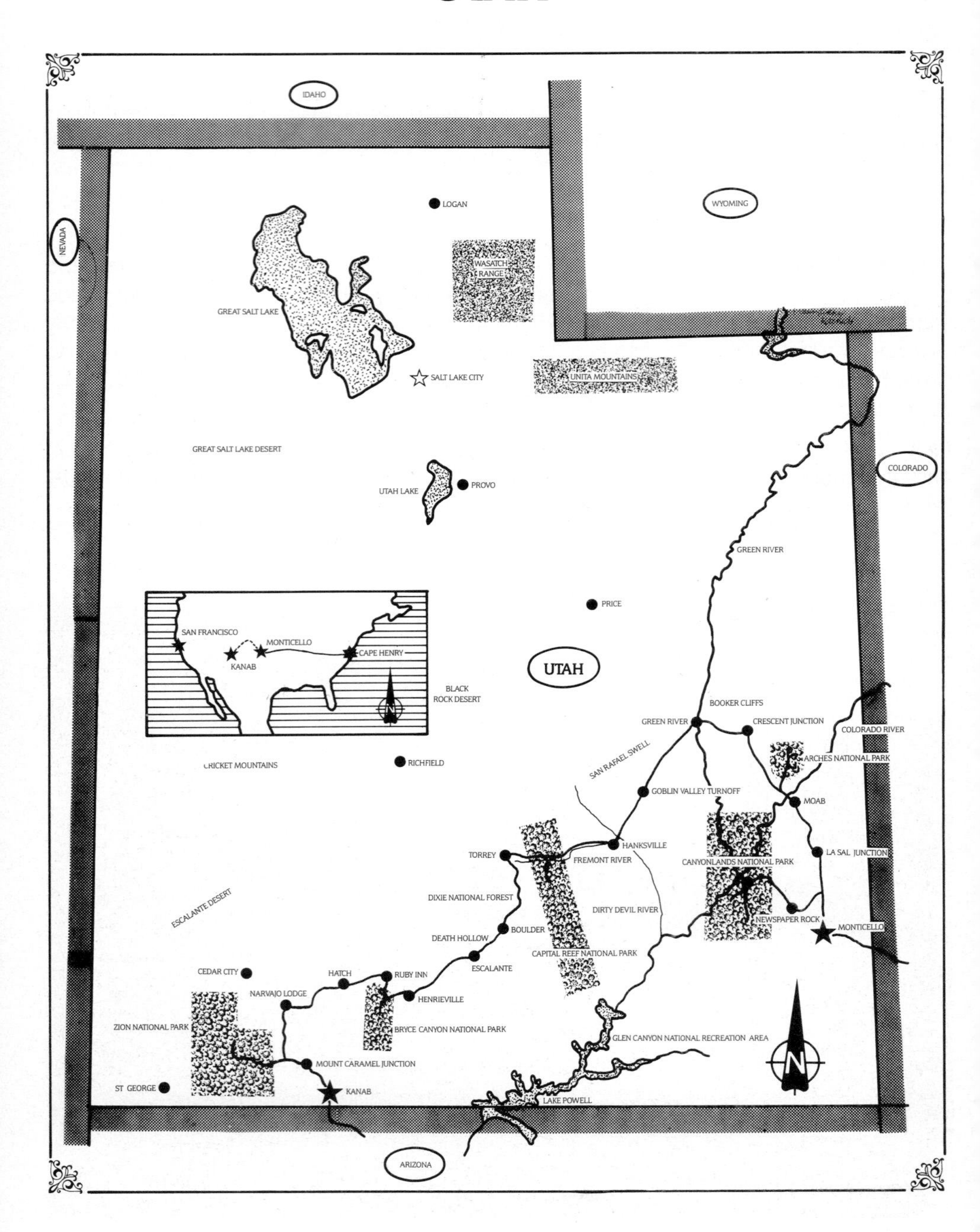

IDAHO
WYOMING
NEVADA
COLORADO
ARIZONA
UTAH
LOGAN
WASATCH RANGE
GREAT SALT LAKE
SALT LAKE CITY
UNITA MOUNTAINS
GREAT SALT LAKE DESERT
UTAH LAKE
PROVO
GREEN RIVER
PRICE
SAN FRANCISCO
MONTICELLO
KANAB
CAPE HENRY
BLACK ROCK DESERT
BOOKER CLIFFS
GREEN RIVER
CRESCENT JUNCTION
COLORADO RIVER
SAN RAFAEL SWELL
ARCHES NATIONAL PARK
CRICKET MOUNTAINS
RICHFIELD
GOBLIN VALLEY TURNOFF
MOAB
HANKSVILLE
TORREY
FREMONT RIVER
CANYONLANDS NATIONAL PARK
LA SAL JUNCTION
ESCALANTE DESERT
DIXIE NATIONAL FOREST
DIRTY DEVIL RIVER
NEWSPAPER ROCK
MONTICELLO
DEATH HOLLOW
BOULDER
CAPITAL REEF NATIONAL PARK
ESCALANTE
CEDAR CITY
HATCH
RUBY INN
NARVAJO LODGE
HENRIEVILLE
ZION NATIONAL PARK
BRYCE CANYON NATIONAL PARK
GLEN CANYON NATIONAL RECREATION AREA
MOUNT CARAMEL JUNCTION
ST GEORGE
KANAB
LAKE POWELL

UTAH—THE BEEHIVE STATE

CAPITAL—SALT LAKE CITY

POPULATION—(1984)—1,461,000—RANKED 36TH

HIGHEST ELEVATION—KING'S PEAK, 13,528 FEET

LOWEST ELEVATION—NEAR ST. GEORGE, 2,100 FEET

TOTAL AREA—11TH IN SIZE—84,916 SQUARE MILES

STATE BIRD—SEAGULL

STATE TREE—BLUE SPRUCE

STATE FLOWER—SEGO LILY

The 45th state admitted to the Union on January 4th 1896, with a population of about 250,000. A land of superlatives and extremes—in the north are the 13,000 foot high Wasatch and Uinta Mountains famed for powder skiing, with a precipitation of 60 inches. In the south are desert and remarkable rock formations of Canyonlands and Bryce Canyon; here only an inch of precipiation falls annually. The State is also home of land speed racing on the Bonneville salt flats. Unknowingly for me, I was about to enter the most captivating and scenic area in America.

Canyonlands National Park

DAY 108—
DOVE CREEK TO MONTICELLO KOA—
24 MILES (2,595 MILES)

I strode out purposefully under the clear blue sky wearing my new boots, along Highway 666 towards the Utah state line six miles away. Two hours later I placed the camera on the top of the rucksack and ran backwards and forwards taking several pictures of myself beside the state sign. Elated I pressed on—'Utah here we come'. The road was little used and lined with Utah juniper or pinion pine shimmering in the heat—it was 95 degrees; back to the heat again!

As usual I carried no water, and after seeing a hose pipe lying beside a solitary house after twenty miles, I couldn't resist a drink. I ate nothing either until I reached the Monticello KOA. My new boots had made my heels sore and the last five miles were done in the old pair. The site was empty and I turned out to be the only one camping there. There was little shade but the outdoor jaccuzi certainly eased my tired and sore feet. The owners strongly recommended the eating house at the top of the road and I went along. The building was nothing pretentious, but the home cooked food by the elderly owner was first class.

JOHN MERRILL AND UTAH STATE SIGN

DAY 109—
MONTICELLO KOA TO MONTICELLO—
10 MILES (2,605 MILES)

My heels were still very tender in the morning and I decided it would be wiser to take it easy and let them get better. I also felt it was time to send the old boots back and could definitely feel the extra weight on my back. In Monticello I checked into a motel so I could spend the afternoon preparing for the walk ahead. Parcelling the boots proved adventurous, scrounging a box from the grocery store and tape from a stationers. I am sure the Postmaster didn't know what to make of the 'mad Englishman' who wanted to send a pair of battered boots home as a momento! The postal charge was more than they were worth.

I was now committed to the new boots, but felt they were broken in enough and that I should experience no more trouble. Since it was a 'spring cleaning' exercise, I went all the way and purchased a couple of days' food, wrote cards to Sheila and friends, washed all my clothes and had my hair and beard cut for $9. Early evening, wearing a battered but clean smelling T shirt and eating my way through a tender steak, I didn't like the laziness of the day but felt I was justified in the circumstances. In fact, had I not lingered a remarkable sequence of events ahead would not have occurred. But that night I was unaware of what I was about to walk into and see.

CHURCH ROCK

DAY 110—MONTICELLO TO CHURCH ROCK AND CANYONLANDS NATIONAL PARK——25 MILES (2,630 MILES)

The first of September and still in the high 90's. I headed north along Highway 163 with views back to the 11,000 foot high Abajo Peak. At first the highway was level around the 7,000 foot mark. A jeep pulled up with the owner offering me a lift, or rather insisting I take one—'too hot and dry to walk', he said. When I explained I was quite happy and enjoying the walk we began to argue, for he could not understand why anyone should walk. When I explained I had walked from the Atlantic, his face fell, and he shook me by the hand wishing me well!

I pressed on slowly descending a shallow canyon, and at about 6,800 feet reached a rise and looked across a very deep and wide canyon. Not knowing what was ahead I was thrilled to see such majestic beauty. Rings of sand coloured stone bordered the view with a few isolated rocks scattered around. I looked through the binoculars at the area and set off enthralled into the heat, desert and Utah's unsurpassed scenery. I didn't know it at the time, but I had entered heaven.

After twenty miles I reached the road junction opposite the impressive solitary Church Rock. To my left was the road to Canyonlands National Park. There was no water along here until the campground 32 miles away; even that is brought in by tanker truck. I debated what to do; either press on to La Sal junction ten miles away and hopefully get water and camp there, or try and get to Canyonlands. I sat beside the road pondering what to do while changing a film in my camera. That done I decided it was wisest to continue to La Sal. I was just about to strap on my rucksack when a car appeared and turned for Canyonlands and stopped. The occupants, Brad and Kevin, came across and said they were going to the campground for a couple of days and I was welcome to join them. Fate had played its hand; I jumped at the chance and we drove to the National Park.

NEWSPAPER ROCK

After twelve miles we stopped at Newspaper Rock, whose surface is covered with Indian pictographs,many of which even today are not understood. Half an hour later we were driving past Sixshooter Peak which looked like a miniature Monument Valley. The scenery of rock walls and canyons left me spellbound, never have I seen such incredible beauty. I just wept with emotion at the incredible good fortune at being able to see this area.

We pitched our tents in the campground in the shade of the Utah juniper trees and set off to explore, aiming for the Devil's Kitchen area. Although not far away, the numerous canyons and rock walls were a maze and one had to keep looking for cairns (ducks) marking the route. All the time my eyes just popped out of their sockets gazing at the rock formations created by water, but with the skill of an artist. Few places have impressed me more.

That night after cooking a meal we joined some of the other campers and sat around a fire listening to a talk by one of the Rangers. She was feeling slightly under the weather, having been stung by a scorpion that afternoon! Fortunately they are not very lethal, and I would be seeing several over the next few days. We all became initiated into how the Indians lived in the area, using the natural Indian Rice grass, the bark of the juniper trees and prickly pear cactus. We all sat entranced as the sun set, lighting the rock walls a vivid orange. It was the end of a remarkable day.

CANYONLANDS

DAY 111—CANYONLANDS AND LA SAL JUNCTION—25 MILES (2,655 MILES)

Brad and Kevin plannned to mountain bike all day, but would be leaving for the road in the late afternoon. This gave me the oppurtunity to explore a fraction of this wonderland, and I decided to hike the ten miles of trail to the Druid Archway. There is no defined trail as such, just cairns at intervals marking the route. The walk took me over rock faces, up ladders, around canyon walls and over them, and along dried up river beds of Big Spring Canyon and Squaw Canyon. I saw no one or anything, just the peaceful surroundings of rock eroded into perfect curves and dramatic shapes, with the odd yucca and pinion pine growing.

After three hours of walking in 95 degrees I ascended for the last time and sat beside the 70 foot high Druid Archway. The effort was worth it to see this natural feature. I took a few photographs, in fact I took more photographs in the few hours I was in Canyonlands than anywhere else on the walk. I hadn't been there long when I heard voices and a party of three arrived. They came from nearby Moab and although they had lived there for fifteen years had never been here before! One ran the High Desert Gift shop and another, Jonathan, was a dentist, although I didn't know it then. I explained my walk and Jonathan suggested I stayed with him once I got to Moab. They would be there that night, but for me it was three days walk. Again fate had opened another door.

I retraced my steps over the rocks and past the unique polyorganic soil that only grows here and supports the plantlife, back to the campground. Brad and Kevin had returned and were packing their tent up. I quickly did the same and we set off back to Highway 163. I glowed with pleasure at seeing such incredible beauty but was soon brought back to earth when dumped by the roadside and Brad and Kevin headed for Telluride in Colorado. With this excursion I was low on food and decided I would have to hitch a lift to the KOA campground near Moab. I had eaten only three granola bars and drank some water all day. It was now early evening. After five miles and with very little traffic passing, I got a lift to the campground.

DRUID ARCHWAY

DAY 112—LA SAL JUNCTION TO MOAB KOA 29 MILES (2,684 MILES)

My new boots seemed to have settled down and were causing me no pain. Since I planned to camp at the KOA that night, I decided to make life easier by leaving my gear in the tent and just carry a day pack and hitch a lift back to Wilson Arch, near La Sal Junction where I was picked up the night before. I soon got a lift back in a large bus driven by a German who was leading a team of motorcyclists who were travelling through the area. Before leaving me he made a massive meat sandwich for me to 'eat on the way'. With the sound of Happy Walking bellowing in my ear he sped away to meet his party in White Canyon.

It felt strange walking along the road with only a day pack on, and I had to control myself not to lean back too far. I was so used to leaning forward shouldering my load that I tended to fall over without it. Wilson Arch is quite impressive but not nearly as exciting as the Druid Archway, which has to be earned to be seen. After 14 miles I came to the well-publicised 'Hole n' the Rock'. A unique 5,000 square foot home is carved out of the rock. The home is a popular tourist attraction with fourteen rooms. Albert died in 1957 before his work was completed and his wife, Gladys, continued the work. She died in 1974 and both are buried in a small rock cove nearby.

It was hot again, 95 degrees, but the heat just didn't affect me now, my body had fully adjusted to its new way of life. Four more hours brought me to the campground and I sat in the tent drinking a quart of milk. To my horror I suddenly remembered all the film I had taken in Canyonlands had been left in the tent in the rucksack. I found the canisters and they felt very hot; the film spools were even hotter. I felt very upset for days afterwards thinking I had lost the film. I took the film to be processed the next day but did not see the results until back in Britain three months later. The film was perfect and incredibly not spoilt by the heat; again Lady Luck was shining on me.

HOLE IN THE ROCK

DAY 113—MOAB AND ARCHES NATIONAL PARK—12 MILES (2,696 MILES) AND 50 MILES BY BICYCLE

It was Labour Day weekend, and like yesterday there were many people around and in cars. I descended the highway into Moab, four miles away, for breakfast. Afterwards I found the High Desert Gift shop and left my rucksack there. Johnathon Isgreen had his dental practice next door and I popped my head round to see whether I could stay. While he picked at someone's teeth he confirmed I was most welcome and explained where he lived. I told him I would see him that evening.

As I walked into Moab an idea had germinated in my mind. Arches National Park was just ahead and like most places in this area was geared to cars and not backpackers. The campground was at the top of the park, 26 miles away, and the only water source again trucked in. I could walk there but would miss the Arches. I decided that perhaps I could hire a bicycle for the day which would allow me time to get to several of the main Arches off the road. Finding a cycle store, I asked if I could rent one for the day. Obviously such a request was unusual, but they gladly lent me one and I left my American Express card as security. I hadn't ridden a bike for several years and wondered how I would fare on this new form of transport. I little knew what was ahead of me as I cycled down Main Street towards the park to embark upon one of the most amazing days of my life.

Arches has the greatest density of natural arches in the world—more than 200 of them—and they are the work of 100 million years of erosion. After calling in at the Park Headquarters and filling my flask with ice cold water, I set off up the road, feeling as though I was a cyclist in the Tour de France. I decided it would be best to cycle to the far end and work my way backwards seeing the Arches. First it was past the huge rock walls and towers of the Courthouse Towers, the Three Gossips and Tower of Babel. The scene was just out of a western and one could easily imagine John Wayne suddenly appearing with a line of Indians on the skyline. The distant view was impressive to the La Sal mountains. If I was standing on the summit of those 11,000 foot mountains the temperature would be about 42 degrees. Here in the park it was 90 and by mid afternoon it reached 98 degrees.

I pushed on to the Balanced Rock; a boulder weighing about 3,500 tons rests on a shale pinnacle and looks as though it will collapse any moment but has in fact stood for years. To my right were the windows section, and the two window arches could be seen very clearly. The road now descended, and it proved a delightful free wheel before the long climb past the Fiery Furnace area to the road end at the campground. I hid the bike in some bushes and followed the trail to the Devils Garden. After a mile I gazed at the incredible sight of Landscape Arch, the biggest in the park—105 feet high and 291 feet from base to base. The sheer size seemed to defy all the laws of nature and shouldn't have been standing. Round the corner were several more arches, including the remarkable Double O Arch.

BALANCING BOULDER

I hurried back to the bike and set off down the road, fearful of a puncture for I had no repair kit. There were few people about, the heat putting people off. The few cars there were stopped, for they couldn't believe anyone could actually enjoy cycling in such heat. Almost without exception the driver pulled out a can beer from his ice chest and gave it to me—'you must be parched!' After five cans I was feeling the worse for wear. I stopped at the Fiery Furnace area and looked around the maze of passageways, which can be hard to find the way out. A little further down the road I turned left down the gravel track to Wolfe Ranch and trailhead for Delicate Arch. The ranch was settled by John Wesley Wolfe, a disabled Civil War veteran in 1888. Their log cabin and coral still remain, and for twenty years John and son, Fred, lived here.

LANDSCAPE ARCH

DELICATE ARCH

The trail to Delicate Arch is three miles long and, whilst the arches I had so far seen were incredibly sculptured, Delicate Arch turned out to be by far the most unequalled natural feature on the earth's surface that I have seen. All the surrounding sandstone has eroded away leaving a sixty foot high arch in perfect isolation so you can appreciate its masterful lines. I sat in the shade beneath it and drank another can of beer. An hour later back at the trailhead I was given another beer before setting off up the track and then road to the Windows Section. My legs were complaining, but I cycled all the way up the hill refusing to be beaten. A quick tour of the arches by road before pressing on past Balanced Rock and Courthouse Towers and the welcome descent to the Park Headquarters.

I was now saddle-sore and my legs felt like jelly, but I still had to make Moab, hopefully before the cycle store closed at 6.30p.m. They were just closing as I cruised in. Like everyone else they said, 'you must be parched and you couldn't possibly have cycled and seen the Arches.' I explained I had, and the owner rushed out for a six pack of beer! Between us we demolished them in twenty minutes and I staggered off to find the dentist, Jonathan Isgreen. I was decidedly lightheaded and, having only drunk twelve cans of beer and eaten nothing, was in rather a bad state. After an hour of walking around I found Jonathan, who only lived three blocks away and rather concerned why I hadn't shown up. Again more drink was thrust upon me and I called it a day after another three cans had followed down my throat. Jonathon turned out to be excellent cook and made a magnificent Mexican dish. His girlfriend turned out to be a Park Ranger who I had unknowingly spoken to earlier in the day. I fell exhausted asleep on his lounge floor, ending a day I will never forget. Utah was turning out to be a remarkable experience; little did I know the adventure had only just begun.

DAY 114—MOAB TO CRESCENT JUNCTION 30 MILES (2,726 MILES)

Jonathan left early for his practice and I was soon back on Highway 163 heading northwards. I felt tired from using different muscles yesterday on the bicycle, but as the day progessed the stiffness eased off. After twelve miles I reached the turn-off for Dead Horse Point, which overlooks the Colorado River and Canyonlands National Park. The scene of canyons and river is regarded by many to be superior to Grand Canyon. Opposite the road junction was a large sign 'Cold Drinks'. I walked up the drive to see an English type garden full of flowers and a dramatic contrast to the dry and sandy surroundings. I sat in the shade and drank four cans of coke. There was nothing ahead until Crescent Junction.

A little further and the road was being repaired with flag women controlling the traffic. It was 95 degrees and they were amazed to see a backpacker. As time passed the day became hard going, being so hot and dry and the road stretching away in the distance. My boots complained and my feet became sore, but after nearly eleven hours of walking I was glad to reach Crescent Junction. The sign said, 'Yes this is it!'—elevation 4,886 feet 11 inches—population variable! All there was was a gas station, store and a restaurant. After a meal I camped nearby. I was tired and wrote in my log that night—'walked too much.'

CRESCENT JUNCTION

DAY 115—CRESCENT JUNCTION TO GREEN RIVER—20 MILES (2,746 MILES)

From Crescent Junction I headed westwards again and, rather than walk along the Interstate 70, followed the railway line then old road to Green River. Again it was a hot (95 degrees) and dusty walk, but the views were extensive over the flat country ahead with the impressive walls of the Book Cliffs on my right. I reached Green River at lunchtime and ckecked into a motel, so I could stock up with food, purchase some elastoplast to help protect my sore heels, buy some new socks and wash my clothes. I had also been recommended to call in at the Desert Edge Sundries store, a drugstore, for a strawberry shake—said to be the best west of the Mississippi. I wouldn't be so bold as to say that, but it was certainly very rich and creamy and a delightful cool drink.

I had decided that to get to Hanksville, the next 'watering hole' on my route, more than fifty miles away, I would go by compass across the San Rafael Desert and cut a large corner off the road and be heading southwards again. Green River is a major halt when travelling anywhere in this area. On the outskirts of the town a sign boldly stated—No Services for 107 miles. On May 24th 1869 Major John Wesley Powell set of from here with nine companions to explore and map the Green and Colorado Rivers. Many said they wouldn't survive, either from slaughter by Indians or death on the rapids. Although several were lost after 97 days, Powell and his remaining men made it and charted 900 miles of river. He was to repeat the journey later, and his work and experiences are now part of American folklore.

GREEN RIVER

DAY 116—GREEN RIVER TO GOBLIN VALLEY TURN OFF—28 MILES (2,774 MILES)

I ate a large breakfast and drank numerous cups of coffee—tanking myself up for the desert crossing—and was walking by 6.30a.m. At first I followed the desert road to the Airport and took a compass bearing across the desert to the San Rafael River to the road bridge. My map was a Utah multipurpose one with a scale of four miles to an inch. It did show a track going in my direction and for a while I did follow a jeep track but this soon became lost in the region of several wash's. The walking was exciting, knowing here you were traversing a remote waterless area and no one knew you were doing it. Crossing such a vast area I felt totally insignificant, just dwarfed by the magnitude. For me it was interesting to notice how I had adjusted as the walk progressed from the roads and careful control of myself in Virginia to the now confident walker ready for anything.

After three hours topping a rise I could see a track below and I descended to it. The view ahead stretched to the horizon and was dominated by the San Rafael Fault. Two hours later I reached the highway (24) and river. It was full of sand and I had been told to filter the water through a hankerchief. But I wasn't thirsty despite a temperature of 90 degrees. I pressed on following the road past the sand dunes and occasional dune across the road blown by a constant breeze. I had expected to see animals and snakes but saw nothing.

As I walked, a nagging problem kept cropping up in my mind. It was Sheila's birthday the next day and although I had sent a card and present from Durango in Colorado, I felt I should phone her. Obviously there was no phone here in the desert and I thought I would try and get a lift later in the day to Hanksville and phone from there. After ten hours of walking I reached the bridge over the dry Woman Wash and sat on one end and ate a tin of mandarin oranges, my first snack all day. Just as I finished a camper pulled up and offered a ride. That settled it, and I jumped aboard and dropped off near Hanksville. They wanted me to join them on Lake Powell for a couple of days, but my walk came first. I was to meet them again. That evening I rang Sheila but got no reply! It was only September 7th, but 3 inches of snow fell on the Colorado peaks. To think I was there fourteen days ago.

THE BOOKER CLIFFS

DAY 117—GOBLIN VALLEY TURN OFF TO HANKSVILLE—25 MILES (2,799 MILES)

I rang Sheila again before setting off, but again could get no reply and I felt despondent. Back on the highway the first car, driven by Frank Keele, stopped for me. He and his family were amazed that I should be so honest on my walk and want taking back to where I had been picked up the night before at Woman Wash just north of the Goblin Valley turn-off. They kindly let me out at the bridge and gave me their address in Torrey near Capitol Reef National Park, which I would pass through in a few days. I would be most welcome to stay.

For the next six hours on the walk no car passed as I followed Highway 24 and began slowly to descend to Hanksville. After an hour an owl watched me pass while sitting on the top of a fence post. A while later a coyote appeared and kept parallel to me, 100 yards apart, for the next five miles. I felt nervous at first, for I had little to defend myself apart from a fork and spoon! I photographed him with my telephoto lense, but eventually he decided to give up the walk and rested in the sand as I pressed on.

The scenery was impressive with expanses of sand and weather beaten rocks in weird formations, such as Factory Butte and Prairie Dog Rock. Hanksville is a surprise, being a small cluster of buildings close to a river, whose banks are a lush green set against the harsh light brown surroundings. The campground, which is just the dry earth floor, turned out to be the windiest of the walk. Large boulders secured the tent from blowing away. My feet thankfully were settling down, and only my right heel remained slightly sore.

DESERT ROAD

DAY 118—HANKSVILLE TO CAPITOL REEF NATIONAL PARK—27 MILES (2,826 MILES)

The daylight hours were now getting shorter and it was only just light at 7.0a.m. I set off half an hour later in the relatively cool temperature of 56 degrees. Again I was heading westwards, but not for long. The scenery was pleasant beside the Fremont River but the mosquitos were a perfect nuisance. After three hours the countryside changed to dry and dusty terrain with cliffs of the Lower Blue Hills and the prominent Factory Butte in the distance. Rather like walking through the Badlands of Dakota,and with a brilliant sun beating down it was hot work as the temperature topped 100 degrees.

It was with relief that I gained Caineville where there was just a Mexican restaurant. I didn't feel like eating a hot Mexican dish with tachos, preferring just to drink. I was now hooked on Dr Peppers and drank three straight off, before continuing. The heat was sapping me but I resolved to get into the National Park to the campground. Unfortunately it was full! There wasn't even room for my small tent, and a person in a camper who had also been refused permission to camp gave me a lift to the nearby town of Torrey. There for $2 I camped on the lawn of the Chuck Wagon motel and store. Everyone was very friendly and delighted to have a backpacker camp in their midst. The owners' animals were more than delighted and Sylvester the cat took up residence in my tent.

CLIFFS, CAPITOL REEF NATIONAL PARK

DAY 119—CAPITOL REEF NATIONAL PARK TO TORREY—23 MILES (2,849 MILES)

I soon got a lift back to the eastern side of the park and set off to explore what I could of the park. The word reef refers to a ridge of rock that runs for hundreds of miles across the desert land of central Utah, comprising luminous bands of sandstone and shale. The name capitol refers to a dome of rock similar to the dome of the U.S. Capitol building in Washington. Here lies the beauty of the park, for the Fremont River forms a lush swathe through the area which is dominated by magnificent rock walls in a multitude of sand colours. Whilst not having the irrepressible beauty of Canyonlands or the mastery of Arches, the park is justifiably attractive and well worth the walk through.

I visited many of the key sites, such as the tantalising swim hole, saw arches, pectographs and the Fruita School House. Opposite were numerous apple trees which were once cared for by the people of Fruita village. In 1937 Capitol Reef became a National Monument, and by the end of the 1960s everyone had left Fruita village. In 1971 the area was expanded and upgraded to a National Park.

I continued on along Highway 24 past impressive rock formations known as the Castle and past solitary Utah junipers back to the town of Torrey. Again I camped on the lawn of the motel and Sylvester took up residence once more. But not for long, as a storm moved in dumping rain and thundering all around; Sylvester fled to a garden shed.

CLIFFS, CAPITOL REEF NATIONAL PARK

DAY 120—TORREY TO PLEASANT CREEK CAMPGROUND—21 MILES (2,870 MILES)

Leaving Torrey I headed south once more, first to Grover and onto the forest road into Dixie National Forest. Sadly the road which eventually reaches Boulder 40 miles away was being upgraded and paved. The area it crosses is remote and reaches an elevation of 9,000 feet with the 10,000 foot Aquarius Plateau just above. The views from the road are extensive over central Utah, Capitol Reef National Park, Colorado River and towards Lake Powell. The contrast too of hot desert with cool forests was most pleasant. I was back amongst fir and aspen trees, and after six hours of walking came to a spring emitting crystal clear cold water. Fortunately I had a packet of cool-aid and soon had a flask of orange juice.

Two hours later, after hardly seeing anyone all day, I entered Pleasant Creek campsite and camped. The evening brought cooler weather and for a change I had to put my sweat shirt on, and after gathering some wood had a roaring wood fire, whose flames soon sent me to sleep. The campsite closed for the season in four days, and apart from a couple in a camper it was deserted. I was only just making it; the door behind me was closing.

ASPEN TREES

DAY 121—PLEASANT CREEK CAMPGROUND TO BOULDER—22 MILES (2,892 MILES)

I had coffee with the camper couple before shouldering my load and setting off through the forest towards Boulder. The views were exhilarating in the cool air; about 50 degrees. By the time I reached Boulder eight hours later it was in the mid 80's. In the mountains autumn was approaching as the leaves were now turning to the gold colors of fall. But in the canyons and desert it was still summer. The camper couple caught up with me later and gave me a couple of cool cans of coke out of their freezer.

Boulder turned out to be an attractive place although the store and restaurant were closed. Entering, I came to an Anazasi Indian Museum and spent a little time walking around the excavated site. The attendant didn't know anywhere where I could camp. I had seen marked on the forest map a mail trail to Escalante, the next town. By road it looked about 30 miles but the trail seemed only 15 miles across flat country, as no contour lines exist on the map. I enquired whether the trail existed and I was informed it did, and all I had to do was to walk to Boulder Airport and at the crashed plane turn left onto the trail! Looking forward to the next day, I eventually found somewhere to camp beside the gas station. Just as I was putting the tent up a motorcyclist appeared, and it was his father who had given me a lift to Hanksville a few days before—what a small world.

Boulder and its surrounding countryside is in a remote but extremely beautiful area. Whilst the National Parks I had walked through so far in Utah were outstanding, I couldn't help but admire the incredible beauty outside them; it was all of an extremely high quality. To me Utah is the ultimate in natural scenery, and from the moment I descended into my first canyon near Monticello I felt the whole area—the southern half of Utah—should be just one huge National Park. I lay in the tent looking at the sandstone rock, watching it gradually change to a vivid orange as the sun began its final descent of the day.

BOULDER, INDIAN DWELLING

DAY 122—BOULDER TO DEATH HOLLOW 20 MILES (2,912 MILES)

Four miles out of Boulder I turned off the highway and reached the Landing Strip. There part way down on the righthand side was the crashed plane, announcing, 'Boulder Airport and UFO landing site.' On the left was a jeep trail which I assumed was the Mail Trail to Escalante; the trail passed through pinion pine before disappearing! I pressed on only to find myself looking across a series of shallow canyons and wooded slopes. Thinking I had followed the trail too far I backtracked but found no other sign. I tried another way but again found no signs. I took a compass bearing—220 degrees—and set off across the slick rock and began crossing the canyons. I was still ignorant of what was ahead because the forest map was just shaded orange and gave no indication of contour lines.

The scenery and walking were magnificent, crossing splendid light brown rock while well aware that you were truly on your own. After four hours I came over a rise and stared down at the 1,000 foot rock wall of Death Hollow. There was water down there, but how to get there was a problem. I tried several possible ways but all ended with sheer drops. After 1½ hours I began to feel a little desperate—it was supposed to be a 15 mile walk to Escalante. I prayed and said to myself if I don't find a way down by 3.0p.m. I must retrace my steps to Boulder.

As though an answer to the prayer I saw a faint trail, five minutes later, and followed it to a cairn. There was the way down via ledges down the 1,000 foot wall. I descended, admiring the beauty of it all. Nearing the bottom I saw a tent and two people resting by the river! Of all the remote places to come to, somebody was here already. The couple turned out to be Steve and John and were most amazed to see someone just walk in. When they first came here six years ago they had camped for 2½ days on the crest of Death Hollow before they found the way down. I said there was a way out, but they didn't believe me. I said there must be and decided to look tomorrow, as I wouldn't make Escalante before nightfall.

DEATH HOLLOW

I joined Steve and John, from Salt Lake City, at their campsite, and soon had a wood fire going. Amazingly, they had seen me walking three days ago and had even stopped to offer me a lift! I cooked my emergency food that night, a Mountain House meal of Chicken and Rice. To wash it down Steve had a bottle of Scotch which soon had us all relaxing and telling the most outrageous stories. A little later the sunset erupted over the area reddening the clouds and changing the rock colour to orange. I reached for my camera and picked up a live snake instead! I didn't bother with a tent and instead just lay in my sleeping bag gazing at a remarkably full sky of stars.

DAY 123—DEATH HOLLOW TO ESCALANTE 15 MILES (2,927 MILES)

Steve and John came with me and together we walked along the floor of the canyon, mostly in the river, for a couple of miles. There we saw a mark on a tree and a cairn a little way up the rock wall. This was the way out. We ascended steeply to the crest before shaking hands and parting company. Quite a remarkable co-incidence, for in the six years they have been coming here they have never seen anyone else or discovered the way out. I took another compass bearing and followed 220 degrees for the next five hours. Occasionally I saw a cairn or followed the line of an old telephone wire. Like the previous day it was all slick rock with many canyons to descend and cross, but walking at its finest experience.

After five hours I reached a cairn and looked down on Escalante; my bearing was spot on. The view was quite a contrast to being surrounded by sandstone rock, with the fields around Escalante being continously watered giving a lush green growth. It was still two hours of walking down steep rock to get to Escalante and by the time I arrived I felt tired and very thirsty. I stayed at the Padre Motel and drank a litre of Mountain Dew. I felt refreshed, but I had consumed too much caffeine and spent a sleepless night! I purchased new socks as the ones from Durango had now become too thin.

ESCALANTE

DAY 124—ESCALANTE TO HENRIEVILLE 31 MILES (2,958 MILES)

Today was Sheila's and my Wedding Anniversary, and although I had sent a card I tried to phone her, but she must have been out. There were no more phones that day. I now followed Highway 12 which passed through part of Dixie National Forest. The view was impressive with little traffic, as I walked along canyons, past Anasazi Indian dwellings, through valleys and over an impressive summit with Table Cliff in the distance.

My boots now felt like slippers, and although it was now only 85 degrees the walking proved hard and dry. Over the twelve hours it took me, all I ate were a couple of tins of tangerine segments. The final couple of miles to Henrieville were particularly hard as my muscles for the first time began to complain. I had simply pushed it too far, but there was nothing in between. At 6.30p.m. I entered Henrieville, only to find the store had just closed—it was a Saturday. A car pulled up, and they too were upset the store was closed. They offered me a lift to Ruby Inn where there was a campsite and food. I was too tired to refuse. The campsite was almost empty as this was now the tail end of the season, in mid September. I soon checked in before feeling faint—I had overdone it. I quickly drank a litre of milk which soon revived me, before putting the tent up and going to the restaurant for a steak.

TABLE CLIFFS

DAY 125—HENRIEVILLE TO RUBY INN—20 MILES (2,978 MILES)

I awoke to find dew on the tent; the first time on the walk, and another sign that Fall was nearby. Before returning to Henrieville I couldn't resit the temptation of taking a helicopter ride over Bryce Canyon National Park. The ride would be my first in a helicopter and seemed an appropriate, although premature, celebration of walking 3,000 miles. After half an hour of waiting a couple arrived, and after haggling with the pilot we agreed $25 each for a fifteen minute tour.

Up to this time I did not know just how spectacular Bryce Canyon was. Over 100 years ago a U.S. Deputy Surveyor wrote at Sunset Point that the view, 'presenting the wildest and most wonderful scene that the eye of man ever beheld.' The engine revved and, once strapped in, we took off for the most amazing fifteen minutes of my life. First we skimmed the pine trees before the ground dramatically fell away exposing the main amphitheatre of Bryce Canyon. Instantly one was transferred to wonderland and gazed at the remarkable work of water erosion that had created canyons and a maze of columns in a spectrum of sand and pink colours. Our cameras worked overtime while attempting to capture such beauty. After the ride I simply strolled off stunned by what I had seen.

WINDOW SECTION, BRYCE CANYON NATIONAL PARK

I soon got a lift back to Henrieville and there, in the dry sagebrush country so close to Bryce, it seemed incredible such an area should exist. I pressed on along Highway 12 to Cannonville and Tropic. Here I left the highway and headed westwards into Bryce. The park is named after Ebenezer Bryce who for five years tried to ranch the area. But the area defeated him and he describes it, 'A hell of a place to lose a cow!' The more I entered the park, the more incredible it became with wall after wall of soft pink rock, columns topped with white all around, and gullies to explore. I was glad I was following a trail for it would be a nightmare without. Around midday a storm moved in and drenched everything, leaving the trails an oozy clay surface. Five strides and the boots weighed ten pounds. The storm had caused problems at the southern end of the park at Rainbow Point. Here at just over 9,000 feet it had hailed so ferociously that the road became blocked!

Nearly 1,000 feet of ascent up the the Peekaboo Loop Trail brought me to the Rim Trail. Here I wandered photographing more as I gazed and gazed at nature's fairyland. Every so often was an overlook aptly named, such as Inspiration Point, Sunset Point, and Sunrise Point. The sun certainly brought out different hues in the rock as it completed its cycle. On my way back to Ruby Inn campground, I called in at the Visitor's Centre to enquire if the trails ahead to Hatch were marked. No one seemed to know although there was an old forest trail marked on the map. I decided I would chance it tomorrow. The two rangers, Geoff and Rod, were interested in my walk and invited me to a bar-b-que that night. Geoff collected me later and, as the evenings were now getting cooler, we ate our hamburgers in the kitchen!

PINNACLES, BRYCE CANYON NATIONAL PARK

DAY 126—RUBY INN TO HATCH—23 MILES (3,001 MILES)

Again a heavy dew, so I left late having dried the tent in the sun. I headed cross country westwards towards Hatch via the Sunset Cliffs. I followed forest roads for a while but soon found they didn't correspond to the map and in the end went by compass. First to Davies Hollow and on to the Left Fork of Blue Fly Creek. Much of the time was either in meadows or forest with the ascent up the Sunset Cliffs almost bushwhacking. The view from the ridge was a welcome sight, being spot on course with Proctor Canyon below and the track to Hatch.

The descent proved hard and through almost impenetrable undergrowth; scratched and sweating, I gained the track. The temperature was cooler now—only 82 degrees today. The aspens were turning to their spectacular gold colours, and rounding a corner I disturbed a mule deer, who coughed and ran off. Although feeling tired, I strode out of the Canyon for Hatch with a spring in my step—3,000 miles here we come. It was time to celebrate, and seeing a motel felt a good wash wouldn't go amiss and a steak to celebrate would round the day off nicely.

SUNSET CLIFFS

DAY 127—HATCH TO NAVAJO LAKE LODGE 30 MILES (3,031 MILES)

The morning brought the return of hot weather; back into the 90s again. I decided to continue keeping to remote areas, and shortly after leaving Hatch turned onto a forest road into Dixie National Forest. First past fish hatcheries before following Mammoth Creek. Six miles later where the road crossed the creek, I stopped by the bankside and was joined by a female dog, who I named Sharlene, after Sharlene Wells, who as Miss Utah had recently won the Miss America Pageant. The dog seemed to like my company, and despite urging her to return home, she followed fifty feet behind. I don't think either of us knew just how far we were going to walk that day.

Although forestland it was mostly open country with the Hatch Mountains to the north and Mammoth Ridge to the south. The aspens fluttered delicately in the breeze, flashing their golden colours. The scenery was changing from the impressive rock formations to volcanic rock, with extensive lava beds. Joining Highway 14 I headed towards Navajo Lake where there were campgrounds. On the way I stopped at Meadowview Store in Duck Creek Village for milk. The owner insisted I have several postcards of his establishment and a hat. The dog (pooch as he called it) was still with me but keeping a discreet distance. Two miles later the dog sat beside the road, I thought to return, but she was in fact tired. A pickup passed and picked her up.

Later I turned onto the campground road only to see the sign saying the sites were closed and no water available. The Navajo Lodge still appeared open so I pressed on. Shortly afterwards a laden pickup stopped. They owned the lodge and I was welcome to stay. With renewed vigour I pressed on arriving an hour later feeling very tired. As I walked in I was suprised to see Sharlene there; they were the ones who had picked her up. At first I thought she was their dog but having explained how she had followed me they said they would take her back in the morning and find the owner.

LAVA BEDS

An hour later the wood party arrived and Steve, the lodge owner, made me most welcome and insisted on my having a cabin free and joining them for a steak. It was the end of the season and they were having a party. I was shattered, but it was 11.30p.m. before I sat down and ate my way sleepily through a 17oz T bone steak, cooked to perfection. While we were waiting Steve exchanged my Meadowview Store hat for a Navajo Lodge one. Wine flowed freely and we were joined intermittently by a rancher who quite incredibly remained standing and coherent after drinking two bottles of Scotch. Everytime he came in the room he befriended me and repeated the stories of his rodeo days, liberally sprinkled with swear words. In fact two minutes with him and I had learnt more swear words than I have in a lifetime. Later two of them carried him off to bed.

DAY 128—NAVAJO LAKE LODGE TO HIGHWAY 15—30 MILES (3,061 MILES)

I was up at 8a.m. but no one was about. I waited an hour and decided to leave a note and press on. I had had no breakfast and had little food. I set off along the forest road which swung southwards to Highway 15 nearly 30 miles away, close to Zion National Park. The walking was dramatic through forest and canyons and past more pink cliffs. Around midday a storm moved in over the cliffs showering rain and lightning while I sheltered in a cow shed and ate a packet of freeze dried bilberries.

Later I passed the turn off for the Zion Narrows Trail and debated whether to take the route, but in view of my foodless state felt it best to head for the highway. By early evening I was almost there when a truck came in the opposite direction. The driver had just been to a store and presented me with a couple of tomatoes and a cucumber. By 9.0p.m. after almost twelve hours of walking I reached the road and eventually hitched a lift to Mt Caramel Junction, where I first ate a meal and a couple of helpings of a delicous strawberry rhubarb pie. There was a campsite opposite but only for trailers; I was not allowed to camp. The motel was full and I ended up walking up the road to another motel a mile away where I secured the last room. It was now 10.30p.m. The last two days had turned out to be quite an epic.

ZION NATIONAL PARK

DAY 129—ZION TO MOUNT CARMEL JUNCTION—21 MILES (3,082 MILES)

I was soon back at the road junction and set off for Zion National Park. I felt listless, no doubt the result of the last two days of effort. Shortly after entering the park I reached the trail for a Canyon Overlook. I followed the masses along the trail, and like them was greatly impressed by the view of rock walls, canyons and arches. Clarence E. Dutton wrote in 1882:

'Nothing can exceed the wonderful beauty of Zion......In the nobility and beauty of the sculptures there is no comparison...There is an eloquence to their forms which stirs the imagination with a singular power, and kindles in the mind a glowing response.'

Back at the road was a shock, for the tunnel section of the road is closed to pedestrians—I had to hitch a ride through, before continuing to the Visitor's Centre. There was no mail here, which did nothing to improve my mood. I walked up the Zion Canyon for a while after learning that the Narrows Trail was not recommended at the moment. Sitting on a rock beside the Virgin River I couldn't help but admire the work of the river to carve such a deep and wide canyon. The walls rise to a height of 3,800 feet and are often referred to as temples, after Mormon settlers in the 1860's.

I would have liked to stay longer in the park but I knew autumn was approaching and I must press on to Grand Canyon before the campsites there closed. I headed westwards out of the park retracing my steps, after getting another lift through the 1 ½ mile long tunnel. By late afternoon, after sweltering in 93 degree heat, I checked into the motel at Mount Carmel Junction. That night I ate a tuna salad which I was told had a calorific value of 450; not a lot for a daily need of 5,000 calories.

ZION NATIONAL PARK

DAY 130—MOUNT CARMEL JUNCTION TO FREDONIA—24 MILES (3,106 MILES)

Leaving Mount Carmel I headed southwards along Highway 89, passing still very attractive scenery, full of canyons and spectacular cliffs. One area was full of red sand dunes and nearby was the Coral Pink Sand Dunes State Park. Nearing Kanab I passed the Moqui Cave, which, although a tourist attraction, I stopped and looked in to break the day's walk. Upon reaching Kanab I called at the bank and had no trouble cashing a cheque with my American Express card. I gave a sigh of relief for I had little cash left. The bank clerk was fascinated by my walk and couldn't do enough to help. She strongly suggested I stop there and see the parade that afternoon.

I felt I should press on but decided to stock up with food and buy new socks, ready for Grand Canyon. I soon learnt that Kanab is a famous movie location area and was not really surprised. Many famous westerns such as Mackenna's Gold and The Outlaw Josie Wales have been filmed in the area, together with many TV series such as the Six Million Dollar Man. In the Downtown area is Parry's Lodge where the 'stars' stay and the rooms are individually named after the stars who stayed there, such as Ronald Reagan, Gregory Peck, and John Wayne.

I watched the parade celebrating the local school's football success before pressing on. It seemed unreal to learn that Los Angeles was now only 527 miles away; Grand Canyon—the North Rim—83 miles. Three miles later I entered Arizona. I felt jubilant to be here but also sad at leaving Utah, a State that has no equal. Four miles later I gained Fredonia and stopped there.

KANAB PARADE

ARIZONA—THE GRAND CANYON STATE

CAPITAL—PHOENIX

POPULATION—(1981)—2,800,000

HIGHEST ELEVATION—SAN FRANCISCO PEAKS, 12,670 FEET

LOWEST ELEVATION—COLORADO RIVER IN GRAND CANYON, ONE MILE DEEP

TOTAL AREA—113,909 SQUARE MILES

STATE BIRD—CACTUS WREN

STATE TREE—PALO VERDE

STATE FLOWER—THE BLOSSOM OF THE SAGUARO CACTUS

OFFICIAL NECKWEAR—THE BOLA TIE

The 48th state admitted to the Union on February 14th 1912 and contains a wealth of natural masterpieces. Best known are Monument Valley and Grand Canyon—217 miles long and between 4 to 18 miles wide. Arizona still feels a frontier state and many people still 'go west.' In 1912 the population was just 200,000. Mining is a principal industry together with agriculture. Tourism brought an estimated $3.9 billion in 1982.

JOHN MERRILL AND ARIZONA SIGN

ARIZONA

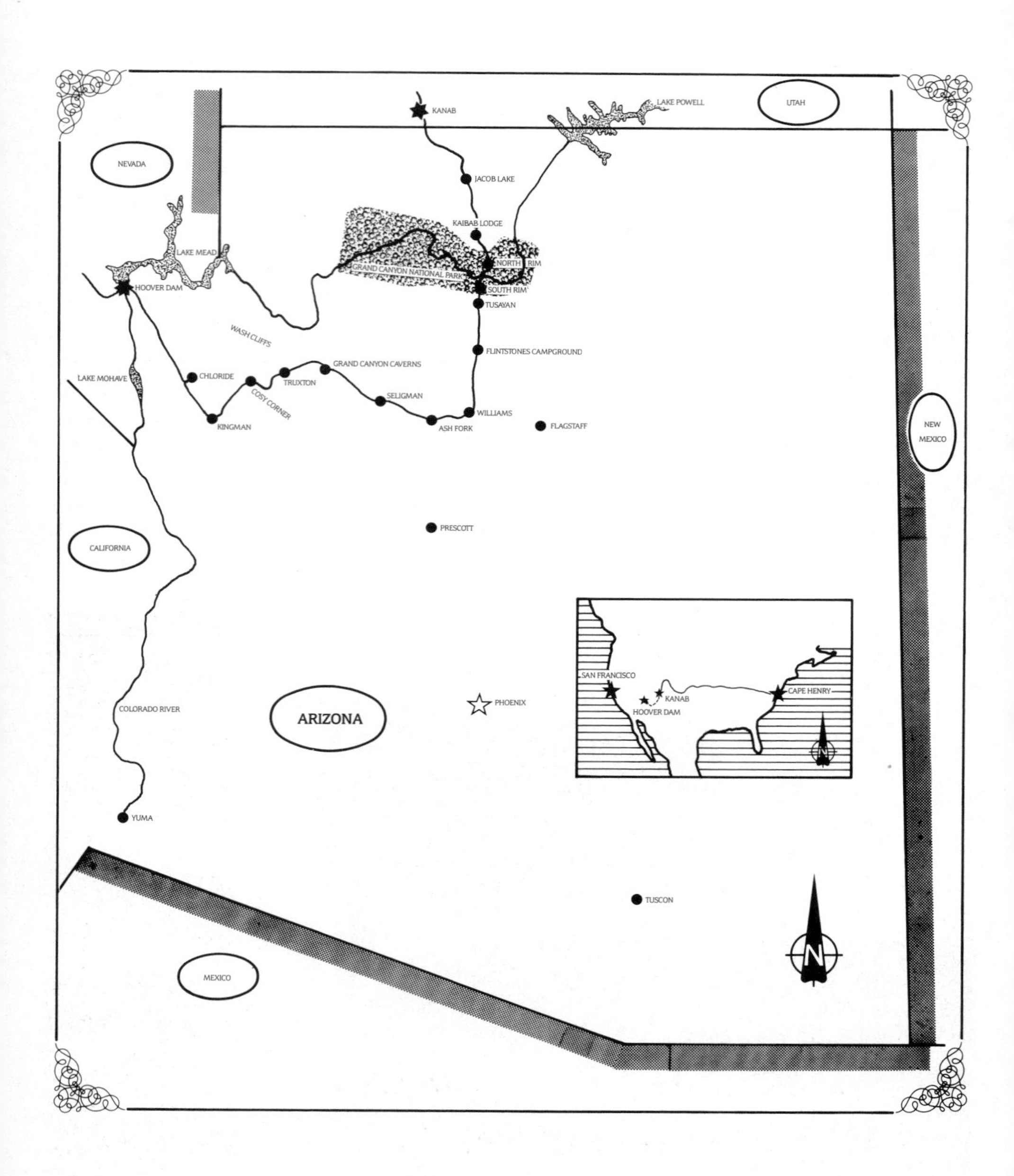
KANAB
LAKE POWELL
UTAH
NEVADA
JACOB LAKE
KAIBAB LODGE
LAKE MEAD
NORTH RIM
GRAND CANYON NATIONAL PARK
SOUTH RIM
HOOVER DAM
TUSAYAN
WASH CLIFFS
FLINTSTONES CAMPGROUND
GRAND CANYON CAVERNS
LAKE MOHAVE
CHLORIDE
TRUXTON
COSY CORNER
SELIGMAN
WILLIAMS
KINGMAN
ASH FORK
FLAGSTAFF
NEW MEXICO
PRESCOTT
CALIFORNIA
SAN FRANCISCO
KANAB
CAPE HENRY
HOOVER DAM
COLORADO RIVER
ARIZONA
PHOENIX
YUMA
TUSCON
MEXICO

DAY 131—FREDONIA TO JACOB LAKE—30 MILES (3,136 MILES)

After calling in at the Ranger station and purchasing a Kaibab Forest map, I set off along Highway 67, south easterly. The view along the road was off putting seeing the road fifteen miles ahead, climbing to the Kaibab Forest. The road was hot in the desert conditions at 87 degrees but upon reaching the forest the temperature was noticeably cooler, helping me to walk better. Just into the forest I stopped at an overlook to look for the last time on Utah—Zion and Bryce Canyon could be seen.

I continued on into the trees, small at first but soon tall pine trees. Birds sang and chipmunks squealed as I passed by; even the air smelt fresher, not the dry heat of the deserts. I was pleased with my performance and my boots had not complained at all for the last six days. I assumed they had finally succumbed to my feet and my punishing schedule. Although tired, I felt elated at being in Arizona heading for one of the seven wonders of the world. I camped at Jacob Lake and fell instantly asleep.

DEER NOTICE

DAY 132—JACOB LAKE TO KAIBAB LODGE 25 MILES (3,161 MILES)

The morning brought a change in the weather, being cool and windy. The temperature reached no more than 62 degrees but I should have expected that, being at 8,500 feet and now late September. My comment about the boots yesterday was premature for a blister developed! However, the walking was very pleasant first through forest before high alpine meadows, reminding me of the Jura Alps in France. I had seen pictures of the unique Kaibab squirrels that inhabit the area with white tipped tails. To my delight I saw four and four mule deers, named because of their exceptionally large ears.

After nine hours of walking I reached Kaibab Lodge and a store opposite. I called in for some candy bars and learnt the owners were keen backpackers. I purchased a Grand Canyon map showing the Kaibab and Bright Angel Trails and a Californian map—it seemed unreal to start thinking of my last state. Perhaps the biggest worry of my route was Death Valley. I had been in touch with the Rangers there before I set off and they advised walking at night, carrying a lot of water and having a backup party. None of which I intended to do, and speaking to the store owners they agreed I was right my way and told me where the water sources were. Learning this information I burst out laughing, for the hardest part looked as though it would be straightforward—perhaps I was almost on the home straight with a little more than a month to go.

Rather than camp, the store owners offered me a bed in the Lodge, as it was almost the end of the season and trade was easing off. I made my notes listening to a tape on their stereo—Rick Wakeman's, Journey to the Centre of the Earth. I found the music and story absorbing and couldn't get the battle theme out of my mind. Back in Britain I bought the tape and it is now a reminder of that night in the wooden lodge, on the fringe of Grand Canyon National Park.

KAIBAB MEADOW

DAY 133—KAIBAB LODGE TO NORTH RIM CAMPGROUND—22 MILES (3,183 MILES)

Very cool when I set off—40 degrees—and I wore my windjacket for the first time for a long while. Not for long; by 10a.m. it was 70 degrees. A little over 5 miles brought me to Grand Canyon National Park entrance. The sign said, South Rim was 208 miles. Other signs noted that if you didn't get to the campground by midday you were unlikely to get a place. There was no way I could get there by then, but when I did in late afternoon the camp was only a quarter full being almost the end of the season.

The Park Ranger waved me through to begin the 17 mile walk to North Rim. The scenery was still meadows, but instead of being fringed with pine they were a blaze of birch and aspen golden leaves. I saw more Kaibab squirrels and mule deer, and in one meadow six wild turkeys watched me pass. I checked into the campground and erected the tent before walking the final mile to the rim and Angel Point Overlook. Like everyone I had seen photographs of Grand Canyon but nothing prepared you for the sight. I looked across emotionally, realising I had walked 3,183 miles to get here. But, the sight didn't make me feel in awe of such majesty of nature. In fact I remained indifferent, thinking it was another obstacle to get across on my route!

I returned to the campground and the back country office to apply for a camping permit in the canyon. I was told they were full the next day and I should have booked six months previously. I explained I had walked from the Atlantic and obviously couldn't have booked in advance. Incredible as it sounds, I arrived on the day of the schedule and could have done! They wouldn't make an exception and told me to come back at 9.30a.m. when they would know whether there was a spare place or not through cancellation. I told them I would walk across in a day and would not need a camp place. They informed me it was a three day walk—one day down, camp at the bottom and a day to ascend. 27 miles in all with 6,000 feet of descent and 5,000 feet of ascent. I felt annoyed that they didn't comprehend what I had done and saw no problem in making the crossing the next day. My ambition was fueled but I little knew what devastating form I was in. I returned to the tent and cooked a meal before getting some sleep.

GRAND CANYON, NORTH RIM VIEW

DAY 134—GRAND CANYON FROM RIM TO RIM—27 MILES (3,210 MILES)

My hands were frozen as I packed the tent up; it was only 35 degrees at 7.0a.m. when I set off for the canyon. Three hours later it was 75 degrees and by midday in the bottom of the canyon—85 degrees. A short walk through the forest brought me to the start of the Kaibab Trail, with a horse hitching area on my left. Here we go I thought, and down I went not seeing a soul. The trail was well defined and every 1,000 feet a notice told you the age of the rocks you were passing and how far you had come, on your descent to the inner world of the earth's crust. I was soon wearing just my T shirt and shorts as I almost ran down the trail, overjoyed at being here.

The first part of the descent, was a rapid descent but after an hour the angle eased as I entered the Bright Angel Canyon and the long gradual descent to the Colorado River. Only three people were camping at Cottonwood Camp and in the crossing I saw no more than six people, so I cannot understand how the campsites were full! Whilst this annoyed me I found the state of the trail quite appalling, for at regular intervals horses had urinated into large puddles which smelt atrocious. To me it seemed criminal to be here in one of the world's most amazing sights and to have it spoiled by this. In the end I concluded that it was the worst trail I have walked along in America.

In the canyon I disturbed a couple of wild turkeys, saw many scaled lizards and the delightful sight of a doe and buck. Further down the canyon it narrowed with impressive walls before reaching Phantom Ranch. This too was a shock, for at regular intervals I had seen telephone lines and now a ranch with beds, clean sheets, restaurant and showers seemed a bit out of place. I pressed on to the suspension bridge and sat overlooking the Colorado River. It had taken me only 4½ hours to get here with 50 pounds on my back. I drank a little water and ate a couple of snickers bars and set off for South Rim, 5,000 feet above.

COLORADO RIVER, GRAND CANYON

Whilst most people complain of the effort of descending, I have never found it any hardship or suffered from knee trouble. Ascending, I just adopt a steady pace and maintain it. I never appreciated just how fit I was and found the ascent very easy, reaching the rim in 4 hours from the river. The crossing had taken only 8½ hours and I felt I had just crossed a Himalayan Gorge! Bold signs at the top said, if you walk a mile of the trail carry half a gallon of water—I had carried none. I left the south rim and headed for the campground and camped beside a group of German lads. Nearby was the biggest supermarket I have seen for a campground and to celebrate my crossing I purchased a bottle of Californian Pink Chablis. I lay in the tent eating a salad and emptied the bottle before falling instantly asleep—certainly one of my proudest moments.

DAY 135—SOUTH RIM TO TUSAYAN—12 MILES (3,222 MILES)

I awoke to the sound of falling rain. I couldn't believe it, and only 40 degrees although it rose to 75 later. I felt tired too, yesterday's effort had drained me, but I wouldn't rest. First I went back to the rim and looked across, tracking my route down the Bright Angel Trail to the Colorado River and up the Kaibab Trail to North Rim. I walked beside the rim wondering at the scene, photographing constantly before I had had my fill and turned southwards onto Highway 180.

BRIGHT ANGEL TRAIL

I was now embarking upon a long detour, simply because there was no other way but to head south to Williams, 60 miles away, before westwards once more to Kingman. Tusayan was as far as I felt able to go, being stiff for the first time. Perhaps just as well, giving my body a moment to recoup. I sent film back and inspected my gear. The rucksack was holding up well although travel stained and bleached by the sun. My shorts were near to collapse, but after five months of continuous use who could complain. My T shirt from Kentucky was likewise travel-weary but I couldn't bring myself to part with it. Inbetween thunderstorms I visited the Imax Cinema and watched entranced the Grand Canyon presentation on a massive screen. Gliding over the canyon you felt actually in the plane as it skimmed the ridges and wove its way through narrow canyons. The rafters descending the rapids and whitewater was exhilarating stuff. After visiting McDonalds I fell asleep for twelve hours.

DAY 136—TUSAYAN TO VALLE—22 MILES (3,244 MILES)

Refreshed, I was walking before 8.0a.m. heading due south on Highway 180. At first it was cool in the shade of the trees of the Kaibab National Forest, but after eleven miles I emerged into semi desert with the prominent shape of Red Butte nearby. It felt strange being on roads again, and a little off putting for they stretched away for miles. The sun bore down and back into the 80's leaving my face yet again burnt, for I still refused to wear my cap. I still carried sun cream but as usual 'forgot' to put it on!

Gaining Valle, which is merely a road junction and a few buildings and motel, I camped at the Flinstones campground. Obviously the end of the season for there was only one other camping. Camping meant you had twelve hours of rest, for it was dark by 6.45p.m. and sunrise wasn't until 6.15a.m.

WILLIAMS MONUMENT

DAY 137—VALLE TO WILLIAMS KOA—23 MILES (3,267 MILES)

I felt tired all day and not my usual pushy self. At first I thought it was because I was back on highways again, but on reflection while writing this, I know it was simply that my own body performance was on the decline. I had passed my peak, and the crossing of the Canyon had been my last major thrust. I couldn't complain—I had seen and done so much since leaving the Atlantic. For the moment I thought it was temporary and headed on along the highway stretching far into the disance and crossing semi desert.

After 18 miles I was delighted to reach a store at Red Lake. Much to the owner's suprise I bought half a gallon of milk and drank the lot immediately. Fortified, I continued to enter more forest and rounding a corner looking down on Williams KOA campsite. The owner, Sue Plucker, was amazed to learn of my walk and allocated me a site shaded by trees. With the tent up, I couldn't resist a swim in by far the best campsite indoor pool I have been in. Beside it was a muscle-softening jacuzzi which I sat in for half an hour, coming out like a cooked lobster. The evenings were now cool but many from the site sat outside with their cans of beer and enjoyed the Kenny Rogers movie, Six Pack.

INTERSTATE 40

DAY 138—WILLIAMS KOA TO ASH FORK 25 MILES (3,292 MILES)

Williams is the 'Gateway to Grand Canyon' and named after Mountain Man Bill Williams whose monument stands on the western side of the town. To the south lies Bill Williams Mountain, 9,264 feet high. Three miles from the KOA and I entered Williams after turning right and heading westwards once more. In the town I stopped at a Denny's for breakfast, my first Denny of the walk! For $1.99 you could eat your way through a large breakfast, known as the 'Grand Slam' and certainly good value. Sitting on the stool drinking my fifth cup of coffee I couldn't help but notice my tattered shorts. I felt ashamed; they would have to go. Leaving, I entered a store opposite and purchased a new pair and put them on in the store. The assistant was amused when I explained the old pair had been worn for the last five months. She wanted to throw them into the bin but I insisted on keeping them as a souvenir and carried them for the rest of the walk!

From Williams I followed Interstate 40; there was no other road or trail and I was convinced I would be arrested for walking on an Interstate, but no one bothered me. Much of the road passed through forest and was delightful and picturesque walking. As I neared Ash Fork tiredness began to creep in. Ash Fork is the flagstone capital and named after a group of ash trees at a fork of Ash Creek, where there was a stage depot. I camped at another KOA that night.

LOS ANGELES SIGN

DAY 139—ASH FORK TO SELIGMAN—24 MILES (3,316 MILES)

The road walking was sapping my strength and I had to strongly urge myself on. First I followed the Interstate to Junction 139 where I could join the old highway to Seligman, fifteen miles away. At the junction I saw the sign for Los Angeles but just didn't register the importance of it. It was reasonably warm, a mere 75 degrees with a strong wind as I crossed semi desert to Seligman. I saw few people and only half a dozen cars passed me in five hours. Beyond Seligman there were no facilities on the Interstate for more than 70 miles to Kingman. I decided to follow the longer old Highway 66 from there. I arrived in Seligman with tired and sore feet and camped at another KOA. To revive my flagging spirits, which may have been due to an anticlimax at crossing Utah and Grand Canyon, I went to a diner for a steak.

HIGHWAY TO GRAND CANYON CAVERNS

DAY 140—SELIGMAN TO GRAND CANYON CAVERNS—26 MILES (3,342 MILES)

I was surprised to discover it was October the first and my last full month on the walk. I followed Highway 66 seeing little traffic but walking through the impressive Aubrey Valley. To the right were the Aubrey Cliffs, still largely a desert area. I still felt tired and had to fight against a strong wind which made the air temperature much cooler than of late. The road was long and straight; at one point I could see 17 miles of it stretching ahead. I spotted a couple of coyotes and watched them through my binoculars, but unlike the Utah ones they remained unconcerned and sauntered on.

Road walking always needed a observant eye, for snakes often lay on the edge soaking up the heat. This day was no exception as I passed several rattlesnakes, one two feet long with five notches on its tail. The road began to climb and by mid afternoon it rained, and I had to stop and put my gore-tex jacket on for the first time for months. I hated it and couldn't wait for the rain storm to pass when I could get it off. An hour later the road descended to pass the entrance to the Grand Canyon Caverns. I was too late to see them that night but decided to stay and explore them in the morning.

INDIAN RESERVATION SIGN

DAY 141—GRAND CANYON CAVERNS TO TRUXTON—22 MILES (3,364 MILES)

Before strapping my rucksack on I took the 45 minute tour of the caverns, estimated to be 300 million years old. Whilst the Hualapai Indians, whose reserve is close by, knew of the caverns, they did not become general knowledge until 1927. Today a major section is floodlit but parts are still unexplored. To reach the main system an elevator descends 21 storey where the temperature is a constant 56 F degrees. The redwall limestone has revealed many fossils, including one of a giant ground sloth who lived 20,000 years ago. The highlight was perhaps the Snowball Palace whose ceiling is covered with snowball-like Selinite crystals.

An hour later I was back on the highway heading first of all to Peach Springs in Hualapai Indian Reservation. I felt nervous being alone entering a reserve, for in other parts of America I have seen Indians sadly the worse for drink, unaware of their actions. It is not their fault, for medically it has been proved that their system is more susceptible to alcohol. I walked through, seeing only a handful of Indians who totally ignored my passing.

I felt more tired than yesterday, both my legs and feet were like jelly, similar to the start of the walk. I wrote in my log that night—'Over the top?' Had I now pushed myself too far in such sustained heat? I resolutely carried on and, reaching Truxton, called it a day.

HIGHWAY NEAR TRUXTON

DAY 142—TRUXTON TO COSY CORNER MOTEL—21 MILES (3,385 MILES)

The walking was pleasant--still desert with very little growth, just views of impressive sandstone mountains—the Music Cliffs and Hualapai Peak (8,266 feet). There was little traffic as the new Interstate highway had taken the traffic away. Slowly the amenities were closing down as Highway 66, one of the major routes from east to west, was being superceded by the new roads. Thankfully for me, a few stores remained and I could obtain my milk and candy bars that sustained me during the day. Keeping me company also was the Santa Fe Railroad, and as the long trains passed the driver would hoot his horn and wave.

After fifteen miles I called in at a store in Hackberry and the owner sat outside with me while I drank my milk, surprised that a hiker should call. She informed me there was a motel ahead where I would be most welcome to stay. Six miles later I reached the motel, Cosy Corner. Like everywhere on the road it had seen better days, but for $10 a night who can complain. The view up the Hualapai Valley with the Music Mountains on the right and the Cerbat Mountains on the left was as good as anything I had seen. Always without exception people in their own area commented that I would not see a finer area anywhere; for once this was true. Sitting in the restaurant and observing the view, I couldn't help being jealous of their location.

Whilst I had not walked too well during the day at least my feet felt more comfortable and were not puffy at night. I inspected my toes and was surprised to find that my left foot had only one full toe nail; two were falling off and the other toes appeared to have given up the idea of growing! My right foot was hardly better, only two full ones; the joy of long distance walking!

HUALAPAI VALLEY

DAY 143—COSY CORNER TO KINGMAN—20 MILES (3,405 MILES)

I could see Kingman ahead, almost from setting off, since the road was straight as a die. The temperature each day now was only into the mid 80's and although cooler I still felt it was sapping my strength, as again I felt tired. Little vegetation broke up the desert view as I passed the small Peacock Mountains on my right.The odd train rattled by, usually laden with cars. In a few isolated places ten foot high cactus trees provided a stark contrast. One was so impressive I detoured to see and photograph it—on the way disturbing a western diamond rattlesnake, who soon curled up and made his presence known.

After eight hours I could see the Interstate ahead and the business area of Kingman, with a welter of attractions. It was like entering El Dorado with MacDonalds, Denny's, Arby's, Burger King and a Jack in a Box. Kingman was the biggest place I had seen since leaving Pueblo in Colorado six weeks before—what a lot had happened since then! I couldn't resist stopping here and checked into a motel. The mileage chart in reception made interesting reading—San Francisco was 680 miles away by road. For me about 800 miles—under a 1,000 to go! I should have been overjoyed at the thought but I simply felt tired. After a long soak in the tub I went out to eat, spoilt for choice at who to patronise. Not having eaten a Denny's evening meal, I went there for my steak!

CACTUS TREE

DAY 144—KINGMAN— 12 MILES (3,417 MILES)

I had planned to walk further this day but my plans went sadly awry almost immediately. A three mile walk brought me into the downtown area of Kingman to the Post Office. I wanted to send four films for processing, and on reaching the Post Office wanted to mail them to England, only to learn that the Post Office couldn't handle it. I had to go to the new one a mile away! The films posted, I set off again and came to the museum area and monument to Lt. Edward Fitzgerald Beale, who in October 1857, with an experimental Camel Corps, crossed the area surveying for a wagon road on the 25th parallel. Camels were not used again.

The museum proved interesting, showing how Kingman had grown from founding in the 1880's as a railroad base to a major mining area fifteen years later. Exhibits showed the life of the Mohave and Hualapai Indians, and a room was devoted to Andy Devine, the actor who was brought up in Kingman. Having been side tracked and learning there were some wagon wheel tracks nearby, I decided to have any easy day and explore them and catch up on my laundry. Leaving my pack at the museum I headed northwards to the white cliffs and the wagon ruts, twelve inches deep in the soft sandstone rock. The tracks were cut by hundreds of wagons carrying ore from a mine on Stockton Hill. Beside the ruts are holes which are believed to have been used as postholes to slow the laden wagons down.

Back in Kingman I set off north-westerly on Highway 93, for Hoover Dam. At the last Motel I checked in, ready for the next day's long walk through more desert. Using the motel's washing machine I washed all my clothes, before eating a Chinese meal for a change.

WHEEL TRACKS

DAY 145—KINGMAN TO CHOLRIDE—24 MILES (3,441 MILES)

I felt refreshed and was away early on Highway 93. The road was busy, but after a couple of miles much of the traffic turned westwards on Highway 68 for Lake Mohave. I had pondered on taking this route via Searchlight to Las Vegas in Nevada, but decided it was better on Highway 93 and would mean amenities were walking distance apart.

First I reached the cluster of buildings of Santa Claus, which was for sale for about $50,000. My map showed a more direct route to Chloride but I failed to find the right road. However, I was walking well, enjoying the desert scene in the Detrital Valley with the Cerbat Mountains on my right. It was a land of mines and ghost towns. At Grasshopper Junction, whose sign now stated the population was 2, I turned right for Chloride.

Chloride is a mining town dating back to 1863 when the first mine was opened here. The name Chloride is named after the type of silver ore found here. In 1910, Chloride became the first incorporated city in Mohave County in 1910 with a population of 189. At its peak during the 'Glory Days' it rose to 2,000. An interesting leaflet guided me to many key buildings, such as the Santa Fe rail depot, a two cell jail and store. In the centre was a battered truck whose side was painted with the words—'Lightning Express—Chloride to Anchorage—Fast daily trips!' A swap meet was in progress and everyone was dressed in Edwardian clothes. I was made most welcome and caused a bit of a stir when they realised how far I had walked. That evening I erected the tent on the 'City Park', on the parched grass.

GRASSHOPPER JUNCTION

DAY 146—CHLORIDE TO WHITE HILLS JUNCTION—26 MILES (3,467 MILES)

After my usual litre of milk for breakfast the tent was packed and an hour later I was back on Highway 93. The road was long and could be seen far ahead, and although well into October it was 85 degrees, making walking hard for me. The landscape was still desert, and after twelve miles I reached the Dolan Springs turn off. A welcome store sat at the corner and I could rest in the shade drinking a Dr Pepper. The Dolan Springs area has opened up recently and many people were heading through here for Lake Mead and overlooks of Grand Canyon. Also situated in the area is the largest Joshua Tree forest in the world. I had seen these trees in the Mohave Desert on the Pacific Crest Trail and, apart from seeing a few seedy looking specimens during the day, it would be the other side of Death Valley before I would again see many of them growing.

The store owner was reluctant to see me go, after having extolled the attractions of Dolan Springs—no air pollution, abundance of sunshine, and low humidity. It was too early to stop and, on learning there was a store and campsite ahead twelve miles away, I decided to make for it. I arrived four hours later feeling quite tired, but knowing I had broken the back of this section to Lake Mead and Hoover Dam. To my right were the White Hills where in the 1890's one of the rowdiest silver camps existed. In the six years the fifteen mines were in operation here, $12,000,000 of silver ore was extracted.

CHLORIDE EXPRESS

DAY 147—WHITE HILLS TO HOOVER DAM 26 MILES (3,493 MILES)

I left early, determined to get to Hoover Dam. Again the sun bore down out of a blue sky, leaving me exposed. At first the highway passed level across the desert before reaching the boundary of Lake Mead National Recreation Area. Here it became more hilly and twisty, making walking more interesting. By early afternoon I was looking down towards Black Canyon and two hours later catching my first glimpses of Lake Mead. The lake is the largest man made lake in the world with a shoreline of 822 miles.

The arrival at Hoover Dam signalled the end of Arizona with Nevada State on the other side. I left the pack at the information desk and took the tour into the dam. The sheer scale is unbelievable and the statistics of the dam wall make heady reading—726.4 feet high, 1,244 feet long, 45 feet at the top and 660 feet thick at the bottom. 3¼ million cubic yards of cencrete was used and concrete was being constantly poured for over 3 years. Work began in 1931 and was completed in 1935, two years ahead of schedule. Lake Mead is 110 miles long and has a holding capicity of 35,200,000,000 cubic meters of water. The seventeen generators have a combined capacity of 1,344,800 kilowatts.

I stepped into Arizona, the Silver State, and reached my first motel/casino complex—The Silver Nugget. It was ridiculously cheap to stay here, and on checking in I received a wad of vouchers for free breakfast, drinks and prize draws. A mind- blowing contrast to the solitary desert walk. Obviously they thought you would lose a lot of dollars on the slot machines, but I never pulled one. I watched one woman change a $100 bill for the unique Nevada dollar coins. After five minutes she had fed the machine with them all without a win. Another $100 bill was cashed and on she went. I moved on to rest my weary limbs.

HOOVER DAM

NEVADA

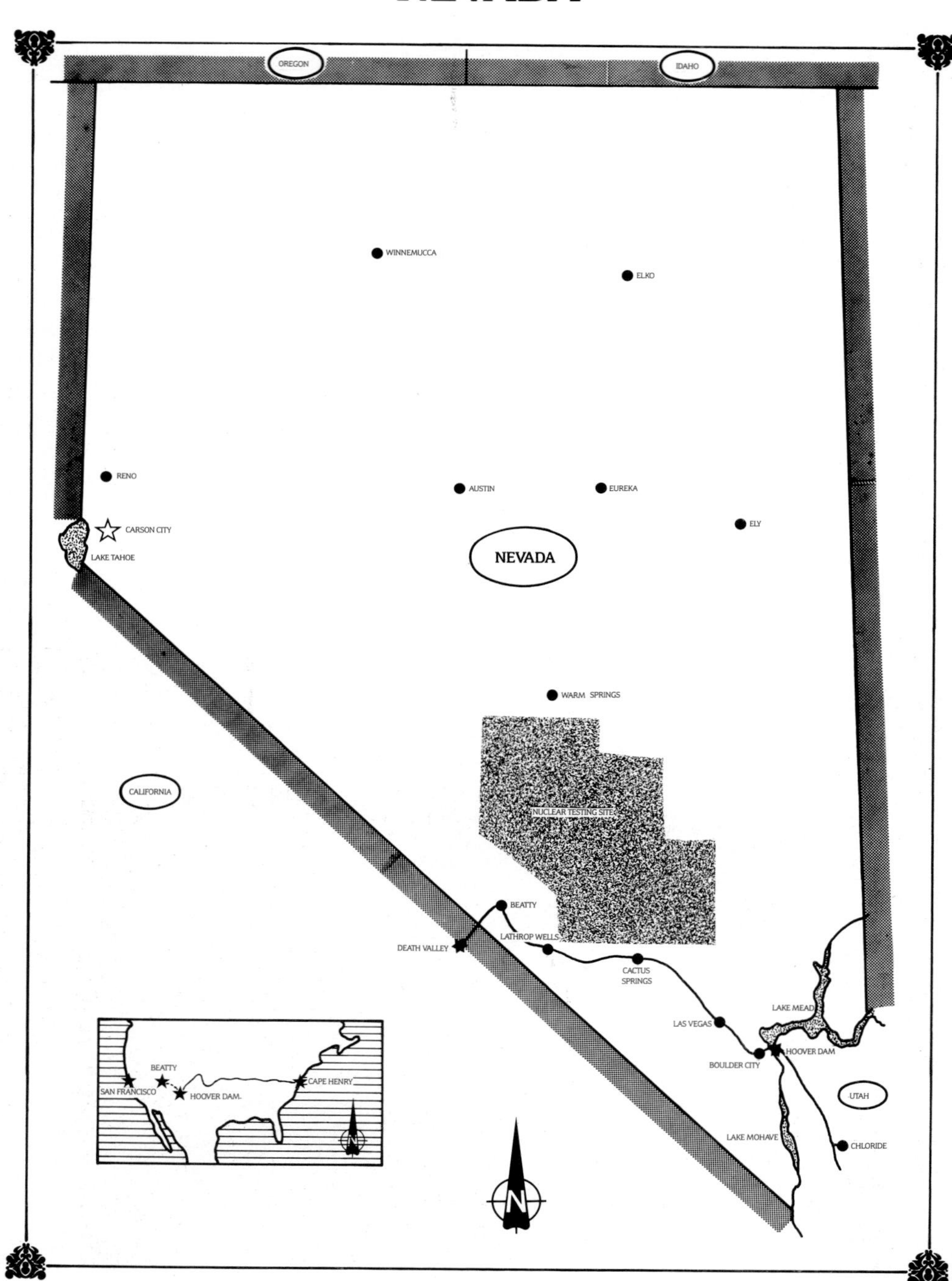
OREGON
IDAHO
WINNEMUCCA
ELKO
RENO
AUSTIN
EUREKA
ELY
CARSON CITY
LAKE TAHOE
NEVADA
WARM SPRINGS
CALIFORNIA
NUCLEAR TESTING SITE
BEATTY
LATHROP WELLS
DEATH VALLEY
CACTUS SPRINGS
LAKE MEAD
LAS VEGAS
BOULDER CITY
HOOVER DAM
UTAH
LAKE MOHAVE
CHLORIDE
BEATTY
SAN FRANCISCO
HOOVER DAM.
CAPE HENRY
N
N

NEVADA—THE SILVER STATE

CAPITAL—CARSON CITY

POPULATION—(1980)—825,461

HIGHEST ELEVATION—BOUNDARY PEAK, 13,140 FEET

LOWEST ELEVATION—COLORADO RIVER IN CLARK COUNTY, 490 FEET

TOTAL AREA—110,540 SQUARE MILES, 7TH IN SIZE

STATE BIRD—MOUNTAIN BLUEBIRD

STATE TREE—PINYON PINE

STATE FLOWER—SAGEBRUSH

The 36th state to be admitted to the Union on October 31st 1864. The name Nevada is Spanish and means snow capped. Whilst Nevada does have numerous peaks over 10,000 feet and they are snow covered in winter, the vast majority of the area is semi desert with temperatures over 100 degrees. It is often called the sagebrush state because of the extensive covering of the plant. Like its scenery it is full of extremes with nuclear testing sites and the world renowned gambling and show centres of Las Vegas and Reno.

JOHN MERRILL AND NEVADA SIGN

DAY 148—HOOVER DAM TO LAS VEGAS—26 MILES (3,519 MILES)

My route through Nevada was a short one; simply as a means of getting to Death Valley and Las Vegas for money! I left early and ascended the highway to Boulder City for a second breakfast at Arby's. From here Highway 93 kept reasonably level to Las Vegas, passing through the Railroad Pass at 2,373 feet. I was walking well despite the return to 90 degree heat. Through the pass and I gazed down at Las Vegas and its skyscrapers and was amazed to see smog hanging over the city.

The road was cruelly long and straight, and after a couple of hours seemed to have made no impression on getting there. On the way I passed a historical marker to the Arrowhead Trail, a former wagon route to San Bernardino in California. I was slightly nervous at coming to such a large populace, but found like Wichita in Kansas it was easy to get into and hard to get out! I was also unsure of how I would react to such a place after being alone and in remote country for so long.

As I approached I kept wondering where to stay. There was a KOA, the only tent site in Las Vegas, but I felt unhappy at leaving my gear and decided to make for the downtown area and stay in a motel. This was the best idea—for $17 I had a magnificent room with bath, king sized bed, phone, and colour TV, plus a free champagne breakfast. Naturally you were expected to lose a few dollars on the slot machines but I never tried. Despite my misgivings I was delighted to be here and, having obtained a dinner ticket for a show at the Dune Hotel, had a good scrub in the bath and donned my new T shirt I had been carrying for the last four months! I even 'discovered' a pair of lightweight trousers in the pack. I looked presentable and set off into Glitter Gluch to the show. It was now night but the neons that blazed out in the downtown area made it feel like daytime. The slot machines worked overtime and everyone was in a party mood. Some had downcast faces, no doubt they had lost their money. The show, a play 'The Owl and the Pussycat' was reasonably good but the people at my table were unimpressed. Everyone was agreed we should have gone to see Joan Rivers. I was feeling tired so ducked the offer and walked back to my motel, leaving everyone to gamble away all night.

LAS VEGAS, GOLDEN NUGGETT

DAY 149—LAS VEGAS TO STEVENSON MOUNTAIN—20 MILES (3,539 MILES)

I had my champagne breakfast at 6.0a.m. and despite the hour it was busy, though many people had long sad faces. Before leaving I walked up the famous strip to see the world-renowned hotels. My destination was Caesar's Palace. No one commented on my arrival in shorts and rucksack as I made my way to the American Express office. I cashed another cheque, knowing the money would have to last to Santa Cruz on the Pacific Coast.

Leaving Las Vegas I headed north westerly along Highway 95, on a dual laned highway. Getting out of the city proved hard, trying to locate the right road and over-pass. I little knew I would be embarking upon the hardest desert crossing to Death Valley. I had pondered for a while which route to take, such as via Red Rock Canyon, Pahrump and Shoshone. Or alternatively via Death Valley Junction, but these routes seemed waterless and I decided it was safer to keep on Highway 95 to Beatty. Although there were long walks inbetween watering holes, I felt it was within my capabilities to make them. It was still hot but a bearable 85 degrees. The other advantage in Nevada is that you can camp at the rest areas where there is usually water. I pressed on up the highway, constantly looking back at Las Vegas and its smog cloud. On my left rose Charleston Peak, which, at 11,918 feet and forest covered, was a stark contrast to the sagebrush surrounding me. I gained Stevenson Mountain and called it a day. I was reasonably placed for tomorrows long walk.

LAS VEGAS, 4 QUEENS

DAY 150—STEVENSON MOUNTAIN TO CACTUS SPRINGS—29 MILES (3,568 MILES)

I really wanted to be in the mountains where it was cooler and I could follow trails instead of walking along a dual-laned highway. The day was the only one when I really questioned what I was doing, feeling tired and footsore after so much walking, but it was interesting with Toiyabe National Forest on my left and a gunnery range on my right. It was one of those days when it is best to keep your head down and keep walking. More a mental battle than a physical one. My boots from Telluride in Colorado, now two months old, were already showing signs of wear and the boot soles were getting quite worn. I realised they wouldn't make it, but hopefully I could get them resoled in California.

After seven hours I reached Indian Springs, named after an Indian Camp and now part of Nellis Air Force base. In the store I drank half a gallon of milk to give me the strength to reach Cactus Springs, three more miles away. I knew I was entering a sensitive military area and decided it was best to put the camera away. In the event no one bothered me.

TARANTULA SPIDER

DAY 151—CACTUS SPRINGS TO LATHROP WELLS—27 MILES (3,595 MILES)

I had obviously spoken too soon yesterday; I was stopped twice by the police as I walked along Highway 95. To my right was America's largest nuclear testing site and on my left a high security prison. Both officers were extremely interested in my walk and, seeing my British passport, shook me by the hand and wished me the best of luck. After ten miles the road became a single highway and it was pleasant walking through the desert and sagebrush area.

There is very little at Lathrop Wells apart from the waterhole tavern and the Shamrock brothel. I didn't know, but Highway 95 is also referred to as the 'Whorehouse Highway.' Prostitution is legal in Nevada and there are about forty 'houses' in the State. I only learnt these facts in the restaurant, for the menu detailed their locations. On my way I had passed 'Close to Two', the Cherry Patch and Chicken Ranch. I camped in the rest area and looked across at the Shamrock. I observed the door for two hours and saw no one go in! I learnt later they have a free hourly flight service from Las Vegas, with their own airstrip at the side.

From Lathrop Wells I had planned to reach Death Valley via Amargosa—Death Valley Junction—but everyone I spoke to persuaded me to press on to Beatty. There I could stock up with food and get into the Valley easily to a campground. There was nothing at Amargosa, everything was closed and no water. The road from there into the Valley had been washed out and there was nothing until you reached the ranch in the Valley; a good two days' walk. Beatty seemed to be my best bet.

SHAMROCK BROTHEL

DAY 152—LATHROP WELLS TO BEATTY—29 MILES (3,624 MILES)

I knew I was overdoing it pushing myself too much at this stage of the walk, but there was no alternative; there were no facilities, nothing until I reached Beatty. It was still hot and my feet were sore, but I knew once I reached Beatty I would turn left for Death Valley and also enter California, a thought that truly amazed me. The traffic was now quieter as the road passed through desert and more sagebrush. By late afternoon I entered Beatty feeling quite weary. I checked into a motel and went out to stock up with food for the Valley and to fortify myself. In one store I saw a guidebook to the Brothels of Nevada. I couldn't resist buying it as a souvenir. The owner informed me it was the best selling book in Nevada. Not surprisingly the guide listed each brothel, and by the authors research he gave the amenities and girls a star rating. It made interesting reading that night....pity I was on foot! The store also sold T shirts and car stickers saying, 'Support your local hooker'. I nearly bought one, but put it back for I felt my wife Sheila would object.

I was very tired—the road walking and heat had drained me—but I felt I had passed through a major stage. My log writing had dropped to writing a few basic remarks, leaving my memory to record the days. I simply couldn't be bothered to write. I was also aware that what I had achieved on this walk was in another realm, as far as performance and determination, than any other walk I had done. They paled into insignificance. What I was doing was beyond the normal endeavours of walking, and this walk had taken my skill onto another level. I now rarely mentioned what I was doing, only saying where I had walked from that day and not mentioning the Atlantic. For the moment, although tired, I was content to be here, battered but ready for the entry into California via Death Valley.

ROAD TO DEATH VALLEY

CALIFORNIA—THE GOLDEN STATE

CAPITOL—SACRAMENTO

POPULATION—(1979)—22,471,000

HIGHEST ELEVATION—MT. WHITNEY, 14,495 FEET—
also highest point in the USA outside Alaska.

LOWEST ELEVATION—BADWATER IN DEATH VALLEY, 282 FEET BELOW SEA LEVEL—
also lowest point in the USA and Western Hemisphere.

AVERAGE ANNUAL RAINFALL—24.25 INCHES

TOTAL AREA—158,693 SQUARE MILES

STATE BIRD—CALIFORNIAN VALLEY QUAIL

STATE TREE—REDWOOD

STATE FLOWER—GOLDEN POPPY

California is a fictional name for an island abounding with gold, and when the explorer, Juan Rodriguez Cabrillo, came to the San Diego area in 1542, he called it California. The Spanish remained for 300 years, and many place names and missions still bear their names. In 1848 it became part of the Union and the following year the famed Californian gold rush began—'Go west, young man, go west.' Thousands did to find their fortune.Today Cafifornia has 'everything under the sun', with high mountains, searing deserts, abundance of fruit and wine, magical cities, expanses of golden sand, rugged cliffs and, of course, Hollywood.

JOHN MERRILL AND DEATH VALLEY SIGN

CALIFORNIA

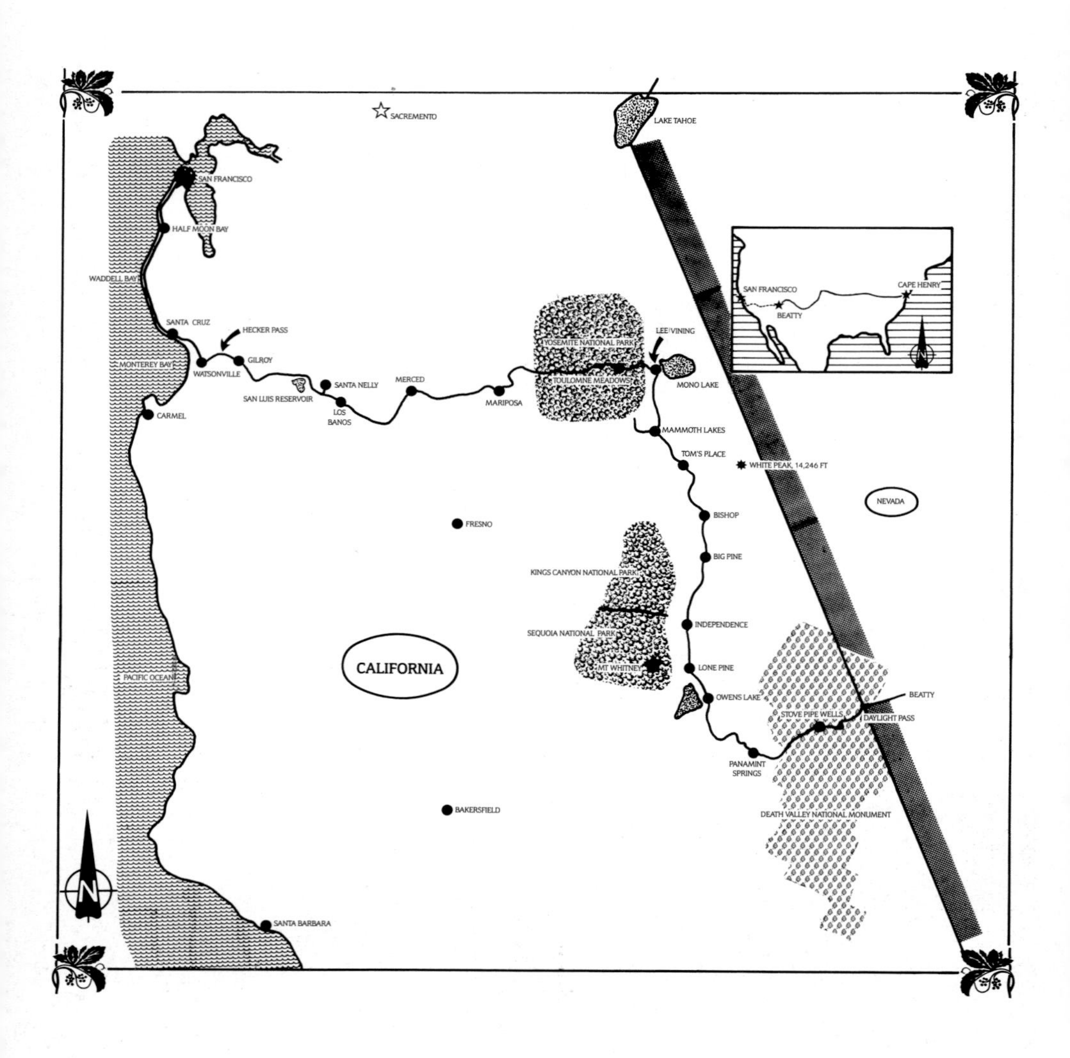
SACREMENTO
LAKE TAHOE
SAN FRANCISCO
HALF MOON BAY
WADDELL BAY
SANTA CRUZ
HECKER PASS
MONTEREY BAY
WATSONVILLE
GILROY
SAN LUIS RESERVOIR
SANTA NELLY
LOS BANOS
MERCED
MARIPOSA
YOSEMITE NATIONAL PARK
TOULOMNE MEADOWS
LEE VINING
MONO LAKE
CARMEL
MAMMOTH LAKES
TOM'S PLACE
WHITE PEAK, 14,246 FT
BISHOP
NEVADA
FRESNO
BIG PINE
KINGS CANYON NATIONAL PARK
SEQUOIA NATIONAL PARK
INDEPENDENCE
CALIFORNIA
MT WHITNEY
LONE PINE
PACIFIC OCEAN
OWENS LAKE
BEATTY
STOVE PIPE WELLS
DAYLIGHT PASS
PANAMINT SPRINGS
BAKERSFIELD
DEATH VALLEY NATIONAL MONUMENT
SANTA BARBARA
N
SAN FRANCISCO
BEATTY
CAPE HENRY
N

DAY 153—BEATTY TO STOVE PIPE WELLS 32 MILES (3,656 MILES)

Leaving Beatty I turned left onto Highway 58, heading westwards again this time for Death Valley and California, my final State. I felt excited, but after three miles I looked ahead along a straight road to the Daylight Pass, 4,316 feet. It took me five hours to get there passing through desert and sagebrush. A sand trail wove its way across the Amargosa Desert marking the passage of off trail vehicles taking part in the Las Vegas—Reno race. After four hours I reached the National Monument sign of Death Valley, and took several photographs of myself before standing on a snake!

I headed on, gently ascending to the pass and into California, although there was no state sign to welcome me. On the summit of the pass E. Walker from Terrebonne, Oregon, was sitting beside his trailer. He described himself as a 'snowbird' who had left Oregon to seek the sun in California for the winter. Apparently many come here to the warmth of the valley. The temperature at the pass was 60 F degrees. I now descended into the valley and the temperature rose to 90 degrees in the bottom. In July it often tops 130 degrees—'enough to cook your brain' I was told!

My tiredness evaporated as I descended fully, realising the significance of getting here; so this was the fabled Death Valley. In the distance to my right the Badwater area stood out clearly, near there was Furnace Creek Inn and Ranch. It seemed incongruous to be in such a geological feature only to learn a ranch resort exists with palm trees, swimming pool and golf course!

I continued descending to the road junction with Highway 72 and turned left. A mile later, and at zero sea level in the base of the valley, I turned right onto Highway 190 and my route out of the area. Two hours later I reached Stovepipe Wells village and camped opposite the lodge on the biggest unoccupied campsite I have ever been on. It was not officially opened until November 1st and today was October 14th, however I was allowed to camp. Again it was unreal being in such a place with facilities and a swimming pool. I went for a swim before eating a steak.

CAMP, STOVE PIPE WELLS

DAY 154—STOVEPIPE WELLS AND DEATH VALLEY DUNES—16 MILES (3,672 MILES)

The morning brought strong winds; fortunately the tent was secured to a wooden post. In view of the heavy mileage to get here I decided to have an easier day and explore a little of the Valley before pressing on. Sitting outside the store waiting for the wind to abate, I was joined by Kenneth Brandt, a sargeant in the Califorinian Highway Patrol. He has his own plane and had flown in for a few days. I told him I intended to walk over the nearby dunes and explore the area a little, and he decided to join me.

The dunes covered a large area and are some the tallest in America. We did a large loop round looking at plants and seeing no animals. Nearby was the actual stove pipe, here the early prospectors dug for water, and to mark the spot a length of stove pipe marked the well. On our return we passed through the Devil's Cornfield, which are really clumps of Arrowweed which resemble a corn field. I had enjoyed the walk without a pack but still felt tired. In the morning Ken gave me his card and said, 'If you don't make San Francisco on time give us a call—I'll send a squad car!'

DEATH VALLEY SANDUNES

DAY 155—
STOVE PIPE WELLS TO PANAMINT SPRINGS
28 MILES (3,700 MILES)

A strong wind was blowing, like yesterday, and Ken was unsure whether he would be able to fly out today. Reluctantly I said goodbye and set off up the road. I was sorry to leave such an enthralling area and only wish I could have hired a cycle to have seen Badwater and Scotty's Castle. But I like to leave something undone as this is an excuse to come back. Death Valley is not really a valley for it is not created by a river, but instead by the upheaval of the earth's crust, creating a 3,000 square mile basin. The surrounding mountains are high, with Telescope Peak, 11,049 feet, one of the highest vertical rises in America.

Much of the road had recently been washed out through a flash flood, and about 20 miles of road had been rebulldozed. Leaving Stove Pipe Wells I was at zero sea level. As I ascended Highway 190, markers every 1,000 foot in height extolled the new height above sea level—a little off putting. Three hours brought me to the Emigrant Ranger station and campground. There was water here but no one camping. I continued on to the summit of Towne Pass at 4,956 feet, thereby crossing the Panamint Range.

There was little to see but after another mile it was breathtaking looking down on the Panamint Valley, surrounded by mountains and, like Death Valley, dry with sand dunes. In the distance I caught my first glimpse of Mt Whitney (14,496 feet), the highest point in America outside Alaska. I had climbed the mountain before on my Pacific Crest Trail hike but I hoped to climb it again on this walk. Incredibly the lowest point and highest point in America are only some 80 miles apart.

PANAMINT VALLEY

I enjoyed the descent into this valley, still massive but more appreciable after the vastness of Death Valley. Part of the road was being resurfaced and the flagman laughingly waved me through. The valley floor was cooler than yesterday, although I didn't know the significance of this yet. At Panamint Springs I startled the owner by asking permission to camp, again it was unoccupied but with running water. I couldn't help but laugh, for everyone had told of no water and gloomy tales of Death Valley, whereas the crossing had been easy. A sign near Stove Pipe Wells had said, 'No Roadside Services for 78 miles west'—how wrong they were. The restaurant was open and I enjoyed a massive hamburger while the owner frightened me silly about stories of queer folk in the hills who often murdered people. I didn't believe him but slept restlessly.

DAY 156—PANAMINT SPRINGS TO KEELER JUNCTION—32 MILES (3,732 MILES)

Leaving Panamint Springs the road began ascending once more into the mountains, providing stunning views over the Panamint Valley. The traffic was light, no more than six cars all day. After two hours I reached an overlook occupied by two cars beside a memorial to Father John J. Crowley, the Padre of the desert. A little more climbing before the road levelled off passing numerous Joshua Trees. Four miles later at a road junction was a plaque to Darwin, which in the 1880's was a bustling mining town of more than 1,000 people, extracting silver. Today it is largely a ghost town.

I didn't linger, for the temperature had dropped. Ahead was the Owens Valley and the High Sierras were obliterated by cloud. The temperature dropped to 45 degrees and I began to visibly shake from it. I put on all my clothing to keep warm, the coldest walking temperatures since the Appalachians. I didn't know, but the weather ahead was almost obliterating my plans. The first winter storm had come in with remarkable swiftness and without mercy, dropping 15 feet of snow in the mountains, closing everything. The cool temperatures and swirling cloud were the result. From now onwards the mountains were closed for the season. Tragically several people were killed; two climbers in Yosemite on El Capitan had spent six days on the face and were thirty feet from the top when the storm came in. They froze to death.

By the time I reached Keeler Road junction I was very tired from the walk and battering of the wind. A group of workmen were packing up for the day and offered me a lift into Lone Pine, out of the cold and storm; it seemed the best thing to do.

JOSHUA TREES

DAY 157—KEELER JUNCTION TO LONE PINE 18 MILES (3,750 MILES)

Back at Keeler Junction the weather was a marked contrast from yesterday, being warm and sunny with clear blue skies. Mt Whitney and the Sierras shimmered with freshly fallen snow on their slopes. First it was into Keeler and around the edge of Owens Lake to Highway 395 and Visitor's Centre. I felt tired all day with sore feet, the crossing of Death Valley had used up a lot of my final reserves.

In the centre my worst fears were confirmed; Mt Whitney and the John Muir Trail were closed for the season, following yesterday's storm. A pity, but after so much country crossed and seen I didn't mind. However, the disturbing news was that the Toiga Pass was closed in Yosemite, just below 10,000 feet. With the High Sierras closed that was my only route to Santa Cruz. Everyone said I would now have to head south and aim for Los Angeles. I smiled and resolved to head north and go over the Toiga Pass; I wasn't going to be thwarted at this stage of the walk!

Lone Pine was like coming home, as I had been here twice before in 1980 on my Pacific Crest Trail. I felt strange walking past places I had seen before, and I stayed in the same hotel as before and ate in the same restaurant. Was it really four years ago? it seemed like yesterday.

MT. WHITNEY

DAY 158—LONE PINE TO INDEPENDANCE—16 MILES (3,766 MILES)

I left early in the cool temperatures heading northwards along Highway 395. The mountains looked resplendant in their white mantle. A little way up the highway on my left was the simple wooden fence around the grave of 29 people killed in an earthquake here in 1872. Three hours later I reached another historical marker to Manzanar camp where 10,000 Japanese-Americans were interred following Pearl Harbour.

I was not walking well, feeling very tired and foot sore. My boot heels were worn down and in need of repair. My shattered state was not improved when suddenly my right knee became painful. I couldn't understand what I had done; I hadn't tripped up or twisted it. The pain grew in intensity and I began to limp. Upon reaching Independance I checked into the Inn and rested, thinking a long soak in a hot bath would relieve the pain. My mind was going haywire, greatly upset realising I was so close to the Pacific. I wrote in my log—'right knee gone funny'. Never having had any kind of knee problem before, I was perturbed and kept thinking about getting a walking stick and an elasticated hose to support it. The knee hurt all night and I slept badly.

INDEPENDENCE COURT HOUSE

DAY 159—INDEPENDANCE TO BIG PINE—28 MILES (3,794 MILES)

My knee was no better and I felt very alarmed. I set off as normal pretending all was alright and tried to conceal my limp. I can never sit around waiting, always feeling it is better mentally to press on. After half a mile my knee seemed to warm up and become less painful. Half a mile later I had no pain and walked normally. From then onwards apart from the odd twinge I had no trouble from the knee. I still don't know what it was apart from a sign I had pushed the body too much.

The road was demoralising, being straight and dual-laned. I stopped at the rest area as I had done four years ago, observing again the sign warning about snakes in the area. I pressed on keeping a steady rythmn, delighted I could walk normally but worried the days distance to Big Pine, the nearest place, would be overdoing it. I needn't have worried; although tired and footsore I arrived late afternoon and stayed in another motel so I could soak my knee in a hot bath. All the time it was tantalising to see the 14,000 foot High Sierras but knowing they were out of bounds. In the mountains here is Palisade Glacier and one I had hoped to have seen. The Owens Valley is one of the world's deepest with the 14,000 foot White Mountains on the eastern side. Here is the ancient Bristlecone Pine Forest—about 4,000 years old, the 'oldest living things on Earth'—and again a place to return to, by car!

THE HIGH SIERRAS

DAY 160—BIG PINE TO BISHOP—16 MILES (3,810 MILES)

My knee did not trouble me as I headed on swiftly along Highway 395 towards Bishop. My reason for my haste lay in my worn-out boots. I had been told of a cobbler there and hoped to have them resoled for the final 400 miles. I did not want to break in a new pair of boots at this stage of the walk. The cobbler was delighted to repair them but said they would have to have 24 hours to allow the glue to set properly. I agreed to have them done and said I would collect them in two days.

I was in a slight quandary and decided to stay in Bishop a couple of nights while they were repaired. I couldn't agree with myself to have a day off so decided that I would walk packless towards Mammoth Lakes in the morning. This, coupled with an easy day today, I thought would give me a little rest and ease the stress on myself. I was still worried about the route ahead as the Toiga Pass was still closed. For the moment I strolled around Bishop eating hamburgers and delicious strawberry milkshakes, before visiting an art exhibition in the local school. One of the artists whose work seemed to capture the mood of the area was Linda Holland, who lived in Bishop. After my initial reserve I let my guard drop and explained about my walk, and for the next hour I rather bored her and her husband about the walk. Despite this we still keep in touch!

RE SOLED BOOTS

DAY 161—BISHOP TO TOM'S PLACE— 25 MILES (3,835 MILES)

With just my day pack on I set off in training shoes in the cool weather—50 degrees—out of Bishop to begin the steady 3,000 foot ascent to Sherwin Summit near Tom's Place at 7,000 feet. Packless I walked well but felt unstable in trainers, even my knee twinged occasionally making my heart stop. However it was good to get high up again and be close to the mountains. The views were magnificent over the High Sierras, White Mountains and down the Owens Valley. I was also very conscious of my performance as this was now the furthest I had ever walked without a rest day. I knew I was retreating into myself, suffering from the sustained effort and emotional problems of knowing the end was near.

I reached Tom's Place the other side of the summit having walked further than planned, but at least I was nicely placed to reach Mammoth Lakes the next day. I hitched a lift back to Bishop ready to collect my boots in the morning.

MAMMOTH LAKES

DAY 162—TOM'S PLACE TO MAMMOTH LAKES—18 MILES (3,853 MILES)

The boots were ready with new soles on; the bill of $45 came as a shock. I was running out of money again! With the load once more on my back and boots on, I hitched a lift back to Tom's Place and set off walking. The boots felt fine and certainly cushioned my feet more from the tarmac, but needed a little bit of breaking in. First it was along the two-laned highway past Lake Crowley and the Airport that was being extended to take Jumbos for the skiing at Mammoth Lakes. In the distance the steam rose from several hot springs which I had lain in four years ago.

Mammoth Lakes had grown considerably since I was last here, with new buildings springing up everywhere. Snow lay on the ground and the temperature was only 50 degrees, dropping to 24 at night. I decided not to camp learning there was a dormitory at the Lapplander Lodge. The owners were dlighted for me to stay and I was the only one! On the way I enquired at the Ranger's Office whether you could get into the High Sierras via the Devil's Postpile but he said the trail was obliterated by snow and not advisable. However, the Toiga Pass had re-opened. My gamble had paid off.

SNOW LAKE

DAY 163—MAMMOTH LAKES—16 MILES (3,869 MILES)

An odd day altogether, being very emotionally unstable. I packed ready to leave as normal and the Lodge owner took me to breakfast; more hash browns and over-easy eggs. I should then have set off but something inside me snapped. I had to explain my love for America and what this walk had meant to me. I opened my soul and said I wanted to stay and live here. He understood how I felt and what I was going through, as his wife was English and had emigrated. We returned to the Lodge to talk more and he even rang the imigration people to find out what you had to do, offering to sponsor me. They said they would send details and he agreed to send them to San Francisco to await my collection. There was nothing there when I arrived there. As far as I am concerned I had for the first time come full circle on a walk. On others they have been long and I have felt a deep closeness to the country and people I am travelling in. It is a sign that I have adjusted fully to the task. On this walk I had gone further pushing myself to new heights through tough terrain, becoming even more adjusted to the country. Chatting to Brian and Mary had released my feelings which I was only partly aware of.

I had to get away, and set off following the trails by the lakes to see for myself the route to Devil's Postpile. A week ago I had been in the heat of Death Valley. Here it was winter with snow and ice and blocked trails. I vainly tried to follow, sinking up to my knees in the snow, still wearing shorts! I knew it was impossible to get through and returned back to the Lodge pleased that I had made the effort to try. That night I weighed myself, finding I had lost 27 pounds since starting and was now only 10½ stone with no excess fat!

MAMMOTH LAKES

DAY 164—MAMMOTH LAKES TO LEE VINING—26 MILES (3,895 MILES)

I didn't really like to leave but the walk came first. Brian took me to breakfast again before waving me off. I followed forest trails due north through the pine trees to Highway 395. The scenery in the area to Lee Vining is very different to what I had been passing through with considerable evidence of volcanic activity with the Mono Craters ahead. I drank some milk at the store at the entrance to the June Lake loop, which I have walked before and which impressed me with its scenery. But I headed directly to Lee Vining ready for the Toiga Pass in the morning.

On the way I passed the grave to an 'Unknown Fisherman' whose grave is adorned with beer cans and a pair of boots sticking up in the air! Beyond was Pumice Valley before Lee Vining with Mono Lake beyond. As it had been four years previously the Preservation Society was still campaigning away to save the lake, which is slowly shrinking due to needs of Los Angeles. Since 1941 the lake has fallen 45 vertical feet. A series of remarkable photographs illustrate from 1962, when just the tops of tufa towers were exposed above the water, upto 1978 when they are now on dry land. I checked whether the Toiga Pass was still open and prayed for a fine day tomorrow.

UNKNOWN FISHERMAN'S GRAVE

DAY 165—LEE VINING TO TUOLUMNE MEADOWS—22 MILES (3,917 MILES)

Yesterday had been fine with a blue sky; today was the opposite dull cloudy and cool. I left Lee Vining heading westwards, as I basically would be now all the way to the coast. I wore just my Kentucky T shirt and Arizona shorts, but not for long. After half an hour I pulled my overtrousers on; fifteen minutes later my sweat shirt, then jacket and cagoule. The higher I ascended the cooler it became. After three hours as I neared Toiga Lake it was snowing profusely and I was frozen. No time to stop, just keep my head down and fight on in the blizzard. At the top of the Pass, 9,945 feet, it was 28 degrees and my hands were frozen; I had no gloves. The Ranger on duty throught he had seen a ghost but I assured him I was fine and pressed on towards Tuolomne Meadows. Snow lay evrywhere and cars were having a problem getting through.

At the Meadows a few people were intent on exploring the Lembert Dome, a popular climbing ground in the summer. In view of the conditions and my frozen state I accepted a lift to the Yosemite Valley. I had been lucky; the Pass closed the next day for good—I had just made it. In the valley I camped at Curry Village.

TOWARDS TOIGA PASS

DAY 166—TUOLOMNE MEADOWS TO CURRY CAMP—22 MILES (3,939 MILES)

The temperature dropped to 24 degrees during the night and I was glad to be here and not at Tuolomne Meadows. Down here in the peace of the valley with no snow it was hard to imagine the conditions higher up. I felt I would have problems hitching a lift back to the Meadows so decided to do the section in reverse and walk from the camp. Although cool, the sun came out and made it a magnificent walk. I was advised to follow the Snow Creek Trail as this had little snow.

Out of all the mountain locations I have been in, I still consider the Yosemite Valley as the finest, but not equal to the rock formations and grandeur of Utah. Yosemite Falls were frozen, El Capitan stood defiantly—the highest granite face in world, 3,500 feet; but captivating all, especially with the fall colours, was Half Dome, a magnificent hunk of rock! My route first took me past Mirror Lake, which lived up to its name, before ascending steeply the trail past North Dome. The trail was well defined with splendid views of Clouds Rest, 9,926 feet. I enjoyed the ascent with the vibram soles biting in keenly, and my feet settled down again to them. Only in the final stages did I reach snow, but it proved no problem. A two hour road walk past Tenaya Lake brought me back to Tuolomne Meadows. Snow still littered the area and thankfully the first car stopped and returned me to the valley. It was a fitting end to my last day in a National Park, for I had seen a coyote, deer, numerous jays and squirrels. The only surprise was a bee who seemed to dislike my bare legs and stung me!

MIRROR LAKE

DAY 167—CURRY CAMP TO INDIAN FLATS 20 MILES (3,959 MILES)

Before leaving I readjusted my watch, putting it back an hour to Standard Time; now nine hours behind Britain. I left walking slowly, savouring every moment as I walked through the valley, which looked particularly attractive in the autumn colours. I gazed for the last time at Yosemite Falls, 2,500 feet high. Then at El Capitan where two Japanese climbers froze to death just below the top. People were still climbing the walls and I watched a party of two coming towards the end of their 3,000 ascent. On my left was the delicate Bridal Veil Falls. I followed the banks of the Merced River but soon had to resort to the Highway 140 as it began to descend out of the National Park.

I knew the last lap was approaching, heading for the home straight but I showed no emotion. The last stunning piece of nature was behind me now, to be replaced by the San Joaquin Valley and Coastal Range. Foolishly I thought I would be able to see the sea, but it would be several days yet before it revealed itself. Buses passed taking people from San Francisco to—'See Yosemite in a day'. Seemed cruel although I didn't appreciate the words San Francisco, that was still 300 miles away for me; for them 184 miles. The Merced valley proved attractive and the temperature, because I was returning to lower altitudes, began to rise to 70 degrees. My knee had stopped murmuring and I was left with a swollen leg to worry about from the bee. I stopped at Indian Flats at a campground, well satisfied at my performance.

EL CAPITAN

DAY 168—INDIAN FLATS TO MARIPOSA—25 MILES (3,984 MILES)

A perfect day—beautiful walking beside the Merced River, pleasant temperatures and found a $20 bill on the roadside! I kept on Highway 140 first beside the river to Briceburg before ascending to Midpines and the descent to Mariposa. I was slowly losing height with the elevation of Mariposa only 1,962 feet. By the river I had passed the oldest rocks in the Yosemite region and almost trodden on a tarantula spider. The latter is supposed to come out when it is about to rain, so I was told, but rain was several days away. The five inch diameter spider proved co-operative and even 'smiled' for the camera. A local informed me that they needed a good chew before you felt unwell. I kept my distance preferring to use telephoto lenses.

I walked well although my boots were now beginning to hurt, simply because they had worn away inside, causing blisters. Mentally I was still alert but I knew underneath I was very tired, and the cumulative pressure of such a walk was beginning to make itself felt, leaving me weary. I stayed at a motel in Mariposa and although there were several interesting buildings to see, such as the oldest Courthouse in use, I just ate a meal and went to bed.

MERCED RIVER

DAY 169—MARIPOSA TO MERCED COUNTY LINE—25 MILES (4,009 MILES)

A few miles after leaving I decided that as I would pass through the 4,000 mile mark this day, I should celebrate, and decided to walk to the County Line and hitch a lift to Merced. According to the map there was nothing until then, and I did not want to do a 39 mile walk at this stage of the crossing. Slowly the landscape, although dry, was changing from the Sierra foothills to plains. At Cathey's Valley, a hamburger store—The Oasis—they couldn't believe I had walked from the Atlantic and presented me with a free coke and hamburger, 'to help me on my way.'

I walked another ten miles to the County Line and sat down to rest, feeling quite tired. Five minutes later a car pulled up and Frank April drove me to Merced to a motel on the outskirts. That night, as I usually do every 1,000 miles, I ate a steak and drank half a litre of Californian wine.

FARM

DAY 170—MERCED COUNTY LINE TO MERCED—16 MILES (4,025 MILES)

After half an hour I finally secured a lift back to the county line. I didn't like seeing a section of road I was about to walk, but had no alternative. As events had turned out I had taken the right decision to get a lift the night before, for the two motels before Merced had closed. My walking performance was getting very ragged. Some days I walked well and felt fine, others I walked largely by determination and struggled to do twenty or more miles. Quite simply I had now passed my peak and was drawing on my reserves to complete the walk. I was definitely enjoying the walk and nothing would shake me from completing it, but I was now walking on another plane, having pushed my body further and harder than ever before. Few would ever appreciate or understand what I had done.

Beyond Planada the highway levelled out and went straight for Merced. I felt tired all over and wrote in my log—'end in sight—horrible.' Merced was quite large, with a population of over 23,000 and the biggest place for days. The downtown area was particularly attractive, being back to watered lawns exposing lush greens and a magnificent avenue of palm trees to the old courthouse, built in 1875 and now a museum. A trim trail nextdoor proved irresistible, but I worried about pulling a muscle at this late stage. I moved on to the outskirts and stayed at a mock Tudor English motel; next door was a Carl Jnr restaurant. All day I had seen pumpkins for sale as it was Halloween. Children roamed around carrying them with candles inside, dressed in witches clothing and asking, 'trick or treat'. Everyone seemed to be having a goodtime and unlike Britain went wholeheartedly into the spirit of the occasion.

MERCED COURT HOUSE

DAY 171—MERCED TO DOS PALOS—24 MILES (4,049 MILES)

November Ist—only a few days more! My performance was very ragged as I headed southwards along Highway 59. Every mile or so I stopped and sat by the roadside, partly suffering overall tiredness and partly emotionally as I began to come to terms with the idea of only 80 miles or so to the Pacific Coast! I now entered the San Joaquin Valley bursting with a variety of crops—grapes, rice fields, apricots and peaches. The heat was more noticeable—75 degrees.

Whichever route I took I had to head southwards to reach Highway 152, which would lead me over the coastal range to the sea. In Merced everyone recommended using Highway 59 as I would reach amenities more frequently. Highway 152 was noticeably very busy with agricultural traffic, and being dual laned was a marked contrast to my almost solitary walking of late. There were numerous grain stores and fruit stores close by, and everything had a Mexican feel to design and place names. I stopped at Dos Palos feeling exhausted.

VINEYARDS

DAY 172—DOS PALOS TO SANTA NELLY—24 MILES (4,073 MILES)

I continued along Highway 152 past a Longhorn cattle ranch, but was walking very shabbily with a faltering pace. Never having walked myself into the ground before, I couldn't understand my slowness. Beyond Los Banos the coast mountain range became more noticeable and I looked repeatedly at them, knowing that the coast was the otherside. The San Joaquin Valley is well irrigated and I crossed two canals, the second the San Luis Canal whose dam I would walk round the next day. For the moment I shuffled on past cotton fields and by late afternoon turned right up Highway 207 to a business area with motels and fast food restaurants. I was extremely tired.

COTTON FIELDS

DAY 173—
SANTA NELLY TO 152/156 HIGHWAY JUNCTION—28 MILES (4,101 MILES)

I surprised myself and was walking by 6.45 a.m. I even felt better; perhaps I had my second wind. I strode out purposefully back to Highway 152 and turned right to begin the ascent of the coast range and cross the 1,368 foot Pacheco Pass. The whole area was very dry and the grass a burned brown colour, against the vivid blue of the San Luis Reservoir. The sun shone out of a clear blue sky and my face was burnt again! I couldn't believe it at this time of the year, when it was dark by 5.30p.m. As if to give a good send-off on the last lap, I saw the rare Californian Condor flying above, and several cars stopped so that the owners could borrow my binoculars for a look. Later, on the descent from the Pass a Bald Eagle floated by, and all around gofers stood near their burrows and nervously squealed to each other as I passed.

The descent from the Pass, now on a single highway through a twisty gorge, was a fitting end to the day. Just past the junction with Highway 156, I stopped at a motel; tomorrow I would see the sea!

SAN LUIS RESERVOIR

GILROY

DAY 174—HIGHWAY JUNCTION 152/156 TO WATSONVILLE—28 MILES (4,129 MILES)

I was again away early with mixed feelings, uncertain how I would react later in the day. To my surprise it turned out very hot, topping 85 degrees. Three hours of walking brought me to Gilroy, the Garlic Capital of the World. I was pleased it was not their festival day! From here I began the final climb of the whole walk, the ascent of the 1,309 foot Hecker Pass. The walking proved interesting past cactus farms, several wine growers and through magnificent redwoods. I switched into top gear and enjoyed the climb and surprised myself at my speed. On the summit was a plaque—Highway 152, Yosemite to the Sea. I had unknowingly followed the correct route. No one was around so I placed the pack a little away from the sign and set the self-timer, taking several photographs.

With my rucksack on I walked a 100 more yards past a restaurant and looked at the sea and Monterey Bay. I didn't register much emotion, just noted it was there! I wondered about a meal but with only $1.76 left I couldn't afford anything. I sat for awhile on the crash barrier and looked at the sea before shouldering the pack and descending towards Watsonville. On the way I called at a store and drank a pint of milk—only a few cents left. In Watsonville I spotted a Best Western Motel and decided a bit of luxury to celebrate wouldn't be a bad idea—thank goodness for the American Express card!

JOHN MERRILL AT HECKER PASS

DAY 175—WATSONVILLE TO SANTA CRUZ 21 MILES (4,150 MILES)

I still had to get to the sea and I again left early, but problems began immediately. I was now on a major highway 1, and pedestrians were not allowed. There was no alternative road and I headed on, soon getting highly involved in a three laned highway. After a couple of hours a police car stopped. Here I was within a mile of the shore and I couldn't get there! The officer said he could arrest me, but since he appreciated what I was doing I would have to walk a short distance to the next exit and there by following Park Avenue and Potola Drive I would reach the sea. If he insisted on arresting me, I had Kenneth Bradt card from Death Valley ready, but I was allowed to continue.

An hour later I was looking at the waves breaking on the beach, and, of all the beaches to arrive at, it would have to be called New Brighton beach! I still didn't grasp that I was now at the coast as I walked beside it to Capital by the Sea. Here I let the sea wash around my boots as I had at Cape Henry almost six months ago. Without saying anything I moved on to Santa Cruz and made directly for the American Express office. There I stocked up with money again and revealed a little of what I had done. They immediately rang the Press but no one could come—President Reagan had just been nominated again! I didn't mind; the moment was mine to savour— I had made it!

I checked into a motel—the Ebbtide—and enjoyed a long soak in a hot bath; I felt quite tired. Two blocks away I sat down to a steak and a carafe of Californian Rose.

NEW BRIGHTON BEACH

JOHN MERRILL AND SANTA CRUZ SIGN

DAY 176—
SANTA CRUZ TO WADDELL BEACH—
20 MILES (4,170 MILES)

I awoke to rain—how fitting that on the walk I should be just in sunshine and now here at the coast the opposite. I suppose now that I had reached the ocean I could rest, but relaxing is something I find hard to do. The sack was once more strapped on and I began following Highway 1 northwards to San Francisco. I knew I was very tired and cold from the sea air, but I wondered simply what I would do all day if I didn't walk. For a long while I just gazed at the sea as I walked, watching the waves breaking on the shore and hearing the cry of seagulls.

I decided to walk to Waddell Beach as I could get a bus back to Santa Cruz from there, simply because I wanted to watch the closing stages of the Republican Convention. As one TV reporter commented—Reagan's Coronation. I lay on my bed in the motel toasting Reagan on victory and slowly getting drunk on a bottle of wine, celebrating my walk's success.

SANTA CRUZ MURIAL

DAY 177—WADDELL BEACH TO HALF MOON BAY—20 MILES (4,190 MILES)

I caught the early morning bus back to the beach and set off in the rain. Half of me wanted to relax while the other half refused to give in. I thought of staying in hostels, passing Pigeon Point Lighthouse, now a hostel. But preferred to walk alone and stay alone, retreating into myself and coping with the transition from cross-country walker to a normal person. This I find the hardest task of a major walk. You plan for months to do the walk, then spend months actually walking and living your plan, and then you have to stop and be stationary. I was now starting this metamorphis and occasionally chastising myself for continuing to walk.

My senses were aware of the new smells and sounds but couldn't quite understand them. Waddell Beach proved stunning with empty beaches and warnings of dangerous seals. Inland were the Big Redwoods State Park with trails, but the drive and determination to explore off the route had now gone. The traffic was gradually increasing in intensity as I neared San Francisco and I became nervous at the thought of getting there. I stopped at Half Moon Bay.

WADDELL BAY

DAY 178 TO 181—HALF MOON BAY TO SAN FRANCISCO—70 MILES (4,260 MILES)

Beyond the bay the traffic grew in intensity and I wondered how far to walk before getting too bogged down in Interstates and traffic. Twelve miles brought me to Pacifica where the traffic was beginning to put me off. When a young driver pulled up and offered a lift I knew that was my best choice. He was full of interest in my walk and very kindly eased me into San Francisco. I just stared out of the window at the skyscrapers while he toured around showing me his city. We called at a store and I purchased some jeans and a new T shirt before pulling up at a motel. Hank had proved an angel in disguise and the motel, learning of my walk, gave me a sumptuous room and at a reduced rate. By now the events of the day had gone too quickly and I was very disorientated. For a while I just stayed in the room frightened to go out. I tried the jeans on again and took them off. The T shirt which bore the words—'go climb a street' fitted well but I still preferred my grey Kentucky one. The rucksack stood in the corner faded, battered and looking sad. Apart from going out for a meal I stayed put that night.

SAN FRANCISCO—53 MILES

I spent the next three days in San Francisco and it rained all the time! There was much to explore and see, such as the fabulous Golden Gate Park, the Bridge, the bay, the piers, the downtown area, the churches, museums and riding the street cars. But I did very little not even visiting Alcatraz. I felt like a prisoner in a foriegn land waiting to be air-lifted out. I was very disorientated and shattered at completing the walk. A massive void in my life had opened up. I couldn't bring myself to relax. I walked everywhere, often walking around Pier 39 and the downtown area three times in a day. I kept going into stores planning to buy souvenirs and gifts for Sheila but couldn't bring myself to buy anything. I fancied a pair of cowboy boots and went three times to the store to try them on, and it was only when I had two hours left that I bought them.

COIT HILL, SAN FRANCISCO

Time did not drag and I can still recall the walks I did in the city through Chinatown or to the Japanese Gardens in Golden Gate Park. One day I sought out the Sierra Club in Bush Street with a view to telling them of my walk, but I lost my nerve and browsed around the bookstall instead. My attitude stemmed from the belief, rightly or wrongly, that no-one would really understand what I had accomplished in the last six months. I was more than humble at being allowed to have seen so much; places like the Appalachians, Ozarks, Dodge City in Kansas, the Rockies in Colorado, Arches and Canyonlands in Utah, Death Valley, and more recently Yosemite, all flashed before my eyes.

SAN FRANCISCO—CABLE CARS

On the final afternoon before my plane left in the evening I felt I must do something, and took a boat trip around the bay to see the Golden Gate Bridge, Alcatraz and to photograph the downtown area. That was my last photograph; I had taken over 3,000. I returned to the motel and put on my new jeans and T shirt and caught a cab to the airport. After checking in I finally began to realise I was about to leave America and I rushed out spending dollars furiously—a western shirt, a black stetson and perfume for Sheila. The boots were still on my feet and just my day pack hung on my shoulder from Lake City. It had been a walk of a lifetime, one that I don't think I will ever better both in performance and content. Goodbye America—I love you—I will return.

SAN FRANCISCO SKYLINE—MY LAST PHOTOGRAPH

OTHER BOOKS BY JOHN N.MERRILL & PUBLISHED BY JNM PUBLICATIONS

DAY WALK GUIDES

SHORT CIRCULAR WALKS IN THE PEAK DISTRICT Fifteen carefully selected walks—3 to 5 miles—starting from a car park. The walks cover the variety of the area—the gritstone edges, limestone dales, and peat moorland. All follow well defined paths; include a pub for lunch; and are suitable for all the family. 44 pages 16 maps 22 photographs **ISBN 0 907496 37 7**

PEAK DISTRICT TOWN WALKS Twelve short circular walks around the principal towns and villages of the Peak District. Including Castleton, Buxton, Hathersage, Eyam,Tissington and Ashbourne. Each walk has a detailed map and extensive historical notes complete with pictures. 60 pages 12 maps 96 photographs **ISBN 0 907496 20 2**

PEAK DISTRICT: LONG CIRCULAR WALKS Fifteen differing walks 12 to 18 miles long for the serious hiker. Many follow lesser used paths in the popular areas, giving a different perspective to familiar landmarks. 64 pages 16 maps 28 photographs **ISBN 0 907496 17 2**

WESTERN PEAKLAND—CIRCULAR WALKS The first book to cover this remarkably attractive side of the National Park—west of Buxton. The guide combines both long and short walks. 25—3 to 11 mile long walks with extremely detailed maps to help you explore the area. 48 pages 23 maps 22 photographs **ISBN 0 907496 15 6**

12 SHORT CIRCULAR WALKS AROUND MATLOCK 12 walks of about 4 miles long into the Matlock area rich in history and folklore and make ideal family outings. Included is an 'alpine' walk, using Matlock Bath's cable car as part of the route. 52 pages 44 photographs 12 maps **ISBN 0 907496 25 3**

SHORT CIRCULAR WALKS IN THE DUKERIES More than 25 walks in the Nottinghamshire/Sherwood Forest area, past many of the historic buildings that make up the Dukeries area. 56 pages 40 photographs 21 maps **ISBN 0 907496 29 6**

CANAL WALKS VOL.1—DERBYSHIRE AND NOTTINGHAMSHIRE More than 30 walks both short and long along the canals in the area—Cromford, Erewash, Chesterfield, Derby, Trent & Mersey,Nottingham, Beeston and Nutbrook canals. 84 pages 60 photographs 32 maps **ISBN 0 907496 30 X**

HIKE TO BE FIT...STROLLING WITH JOHN John Merrill's personal guide to walking in the countryside to keep fit and healthy. He describes what equipment to use, where to go, how to map read, use a compass and what to do about blisters! 36 pages 23 photos 2 sketches 3 charts **ISBN 0 907496 19 9**

CHALLENGE WALKS

JOHN MERRILL'S PEAK DISTRICT CHALLENGE WALK A 25 mile circular walk from Bakewell, across valleys and heights involving 3,700 feet of ascent. More than 2,000 people have already completed the walk. A badge and completion certificate is available to those who complete. 32 pages 18 photographs 9 maps **ISBN 0 907496 18 0**

JOHN MERRILL'S YORKSHIRE DALES CHALLENGE WALK A 23 mile circular walk from Kettlewell in the heart of the Dales. The route combines mountain, moorlands, limestone country and dale walking with 3,600 feet of ascent. A badge and certificate is available to those who complete the route. 32 pages 16 photographs 8 maps **ISBN 0 907496 28 8**

JOHN MERRILL'S NORTH YORKSHIRE MOORS CHALLENGE WALK A 24 mile circular walk from Goathland in the heart of the moors. The route combines moorland, river valley and coastal walking and uses Robin Hood's Bay as the half way point. Involves 2,000 feet of ascent and a badge and certificate is available to those who complete. 32 pages 18 photographs 9 maps **ISBN 0 907496 36 9**

THE RIVER'S WAY A two day walk of 43 miles, down the length of the Peak District National Park. Inaugurated and created by John, the walk starts at Edale, the end of the Pennine Way, and ends at Ilam. Numerous hostels, campgrounds,B&B, and pubs lie on the route, as you follow the five main river systems of the Peak—Noe, Derwent, Wye, Dove, and Manifold. 52 pages 35 photographs 7 maps **ISBN 0 907496 08 3**

PEAK DISTRICT: HIGH LEVEL ROUTE A hard 90 mile, weeks walk, around the Peak District, starting from Matlock. As the title implies the walk keeps to high ground while illustrating the dramatic landscape of the Peak District.The walk was inaugurated and created by John and is used by him for training for his major walks! 60 pages 31 photographs 13 maps **ISBN 0 907496 10 5**

PEAK DISTRICT MARATHONS The first reference book to gather together all the major and classical long walks of the Peak District between 25 and 50 miles long. Many are challenge walks with badges and completion cards for those who complete. The longest walk—280 miles—inaugurated by John is around the entire Derbyshire boundary. Each walk has a general map, accommodation list, and details of what guides and maps are needed. 56 pages 20 photographs 20 maps **ISBN 0 907496 13 X**

HISTORICAL GUIDES

WINSTER—A VISITOR'S GUIDE A detailed look at a former lead mining community which still retains a Morris dancing team and annual pancake races. A two mile walk brings you to many historical buildings including the 17th century Market House. Illustrated by old photographs. 20 pages 21 photographs 1 map **ISBN 0 907496 21 0**

DERBYSHIRE INNS The first book to tell the story behind more than 150 inns in the Peak District and Derbyshire area. With details of legends, murders and historical anecdotes, the book gives added pleasure or impetus to explore the pubs of the region. Profusely illustrated with 65 photographs and a brief history of brewing in Derbyshire. 68 pages 57 photographs 5 maps **ISBN 0 907496 11 3**

100 HALLS AND CASTLES OF THE PEAK DISTRICT AND DERBYSHIRE A visitor's guide to the principal historical buildings of the region. Many are open to the public and the guide describes the history of the building from the Domesday Book to the present time.The book is illustrated by 120 photographs and makes an excellent souvenir gift of one of England's finest architectural areas. 120 pages 116 photographs 4 maps **ISBN 0 907496 23 7**

TOURING THE PEAK DISTRICT AND DERBYSHIRE Twenty circular routes of about 50 miles for the motorist or cyclist. Each route has a set theme, such as the gritstone edges or in the steps of Mary, Queen of Scots. Deatiled maps for each route and fifty photographs make this a useful companion to the Peak District/Derbyshire area. 76 pages 45 photographs 20 maps **ISBN 0 907496 22 9**

JOHN'S MARATHON WALKS

EMERALD COAST WALK The story of John's walk up the total length of the west coast of Ireland and exploration of more than fifty islands—1,600 miles. 132 pages 32 photographs 12 maps
ISBN 0 907496 02 4

TURN RIGHT AT LAND'S END In 1978 John Merrill became the first person to walk the entire coastline of Britain—6,824 miles in ten months. The book details the route, how he ascended our three major mountains and how he found a wife. Included are more than 200 photographs he took on the walk, which is also a unique guide to our coastline. 246 pages 214 photographs 10 maps
ISBN 0 907496 24 5

WITH MUSTARD ON MY BACK John has gathered together the stories of his first decade of walking—1970-1980. Here is a collection of unique walks in Britain, from a 2,000 mile walk linking the ten National Parks of England and Wales together to a 450 mile walk from Norwich to Durham.
ISBN 0 907496 27 X

TURN RIGHT AT DEATH VALLEY During the summer of 1984, John walked coast to coast across America, a distance of 4,226 miles in 177 days. Few have walked across and none have taken so difficult a route. He crossed all the main mountain ranges, climbed 14,000 foot mountains, crossed deserts in 100 degrees, walked rim to rim of the Grand Canyon in 8½ hours, and crossed the famed Death Valley.The walk is without parallel and the story is the remarkable tale of this unique adventure.
ISBN 0 907496 26 1

FORTHCOMING TITLES—

SHORT CIRCULAR WALKS IN THE STAFFORDSHIRE MOORLANDS
ARKWRIGHT OF CROMFORD
CANAL WALKS VOL.2—DERBYSHIRE, CHESHIRE AND STAFFORDSHIRE
CANAL WALKS VOL.3—DERBYSHIRE, LEICESTERSHIRE AND LINCOLNSHIRE
THE LITTLE JOHN CHALLENGE WALK